THE WORD ON THE BASICS OF CHRISTIANITY

JIM BURNS

THE NATIONAL INSTITUTE OF YOUTH MINISTRY

Gospel Light

Gospel Light is an evangelical Christian publisher dedicated to serving the local church. We believe God's vision for Gospel Light is to provide church leaders with biblical, user-friendly materials that will help them evangelize, disciple and minister to children, youth and families.

We hope this Gospel Light resource will help you discover biblical truth for your own life and help you minister to youth. God bless you in your work.

For a free catalog of resources from Gospel Light please contact your Christian supplier or call 1-800-4-GOSPEL.

PUBLISHING STAFF
Jean Daly, Editor
Kyle Duncan, Editorial Director
Gary S. Greig, Ph.D., Editor in Chief
Joey O'Connor, Contributing Writer

ISBN 0-8307-1644-0
© 1994 Jim Burns
All rights reserved.
Printed in U.S.A.

How to Make Clean Copies from This Book

You may make copies of portions of this book with a clean conscience if:

- you (or someone in your organization) are the original purchaser;
- you are using the copies you make for a noncommercial purpose (such as teaching or promoting your ministry) within your church or organization;
- you follow the instructions provided in this book.

However, it is ILLEGAL for you to make copies if:

- you are using the material to promote, advertise or sell a product or service other than for ministry fund-raising;
- you are using the material in or on a product for sale;
- you or your organization are **not** the original purchaser of this book.

By following these guidelines you help us keep our products affordable.

Thank you,

Gospel Light

PRAISE FOR YOUTHBUILDERS

I deeply respect and appreciate the groundwork Jim Burns has prepared for true teenage discernment. *YouthBuilders* is timeless in the sense that the framework has made it possible to plug into any society, at any point in time, and to proceed to discuss, experience and arrive at sincere moral and Christian conclusions that will lead to growth and life changes. Reaching young people may be more difficult today than ever before, but God's grace is alive and well in Jim Burns and this wonderful curriculum.
Fr. Angelo J. Artemas, Youth Ministry Director, Greek Orthodox Archdiocese of North and South America

Jim Burns' work represents his integrity and intelligence, along with his heart for kids. *YouthBuilders* will change some lives and save many others.
Stephen Arterburn, Cofounder, The Minirth-Meier New Life Clinics

I heartily recommend Jim Burns's *Youth-Builders Group Bible Studies* because they are leader-friendly tools that are ready-to-use in youth groups and Sunday School classes. Jim addresses the tough questions that students are genuinely facing every day and, through his engaging style, challenges young people to make their own decisions to move from their current opinions to God's convictions taught in the Bible. Every youth group will benefit from this excellent curriculum.
Paul Borthwick, Minister of Missions, Grace Chapel

Jim Burns recognizes the fact that small groups are where life change happens. In this study he has captured the essence of that value. Further, Jim has given much thought to shaping this very effective material into a usable tool that serves the parent, leader and student.
Bo Boshers, Executive Director, Student Impact, Willow Creek Community Church

It is about time that someone who knows kids, understands kids and works with kids writes youth curriculum that youth workers, both volunteer and professional, can use. Jim Burns's *YouthBuilders Group Bible Studies* is the curriculum that youth ministry has been waiting a long time for.
Ridge Burns, President, The Center for Student Missions

There are very few people in the world who know how to communicate life-changing truth effectively to teens. Jim Burns is one of the best. *YouthBuilders Group Bible Studies* puts handles on those skills and makes them available to everyone. These studies are biblically sound, hands-on practical and just plain fun. This one gets a five-star endorsement—which isn't bad since there are only four stars to start with.
Ken Davis, President, Dynamic Communications

For years, I've been looking for a youth curriculum like the *YouthBuilders Group Bible Studies*. Here, Jim Burns provides youth workers with an indispensable tool that accomplishes two things. First, it tackles a number of tough teen issues. Secondly, it strikes the perfect balance between solid biblical insight and practical application techniques for group settings.
Bob DeMoss, Youth Culture Specialist, Focus on the Family

Jim Burns has a way of being creative without being "hokey." *YouthBuilders Group Bible Studies* takes the age-old model of curriculum and gives it a new look with tools such as the Bible *Tuck-in™* and Parent Page. Give this new resource a try and you'll see that Jim shoots straight forward on tough issues. The *YouthBuilders* series is great for leading small group discussions as well as teaching a large class of junior high or high school students. The Parent Page will help you get support from your parents in that they will understand the topics you are dealing with in your group. Put Jim's years of experience to work for you by equipping yourself with this quality material.
Curt Gibson, Pastor to Junior High, First Church of the Nazarene of Pasadena

Once again, Jim Burns has managed to handle very timely issues with just the right touch. His *YouthBuilders Group Bible Studies* succeeds in teaching solid biblical values without being stuffy or preachy. The format is user-friendly, designed to stimulate high involvement and deep discussion. Especially impressive is the Parent Page, a long overdue tool to help parents become part of the Christian education loop. I look forward to using it with my kids!
David M. Hughes, Pastor, First Baptist Church, Winston-Salem

What do you get when you combine a deep love for teens, over 20 years' experience in youth ministry and an excellent writer? You get Jim Burns's *YouthBuilders* series! This stuff has absolutely hit the nail on the head. Quality Sunday School and small group material is tough to come by these days, but Jim has put every ounce of creativity he has into these books.
Greg Johnson, author of *Getting Ready for the Guy/Girl Thing* and *Keeping Your Cool While Sharing Your Faith*

The practicing youth worker always needs more ammunition. Here is a whole book full of practical, usable resources for those facing kids face-to-face. *YouthBuilders Group Bible Studies* will get that blank stare off the faces of kids in your youth meeting!
Jay Kesler, President, Taylor University

I couldn't be more excited about the *YouthBuilders Group Bible Studies*. It couldn't have arrived at a more needed time. Spiritually we approach the future engaged in war with young people taking direct hits from the devil. This series will practically help teens who feel partially equipped to "put on the whole armor of God."
Mike MacIntosh, Pastor, Horizon Christian Fellowship

My ministry takes me to the lost kids in our nation's cities where youth games and activities are often irrelevant and plain Bible knowledge for the sake of learning is unattractive. Young people need the information necessary to make wise decisions related to everyday problems. *YouthBuilders* will help many young people integrate their faith into everyday life, which after all is our goal as youth workers.
Miles McPherson, President, Project Intercept

Jim Burns's passion for teens, youth workers and parents of teens is evident in the *YouthBuilders Group Bible Studies*. He has a gift of presenting biblical truths on a level teens will fully understand, and youth workers and parents can easily communicate.
Al Menconi, President, Al Menconi Ministries

Youth ministry curriculum is often directed to only one spoke of the wheel of youth ministry—the adolescent. Not so with this material! Jim has enlarged the education circle, including information for the adolescent, the parent and the youth worker. *YouthBuilders Group Bible Studies* is youth and family ministry-oriented material at its best.
Helen Musick, Instructor of Youth Ministry, Asbury Seminary

Finally, a Bible study that has it all! It's action-packed, practical and biblical; but that's only the beginning. *YouthBuilders* involves students in the Scriptures. It's relational, interactive and leads kids towards lifestyle changes. The unique aspect is a page for parents, something that's usually missing from adolescent curriculum. Jim Burns has outdone himself. This isn't a home run—it's a grand slam!
Dr. David Olshine, Director of Youth Ministries, Columbia International University

Here is a thoughtful and relevant curriculum designed to meet the needs of youth workers, parents and students. It's creative, interactive and biblical—and with Jim Burns's name on it, you know you're getting a quality resource.
Laurie Polich, Youth Director, First Presbyterian Church of Berkeley

Jim Burns's *YouthBuilders Group Bible Studies* will be a tremendous ministry resource for years to come. Jim's years of experience and love for kids are evident on every page. This is a resource that is user-friendly, learner-centered and intentionally biblical. I love having a resource like this that I can recommend to youth ministry volunteers and professionals! I especially like the idea of adding a Parent Page in each session. Neat idea!
Duffy Robbins, Chairman, Department of Youth Ministry, Eastern College

Relevant! Cutting edge! The flow gets kids involved in God's Word and makes it come alive in their lives.
Barry St. Clair, Executive Director, Reach Out Ministries

In 10 years of youth ministry I've never used a curriculum because I've never found anything that actively involves students in the learning process, speaks to young people where they are and challenges them with biblical truth—I'll use this! *YouthBuilders Group Bible Studies* is a complete curriculum that is helpful to parents, youth leaders and, most importantly, today's youth.
Glenn Schroeder, Youth and Young Adult Ministries, Vineyard Christian Fellowship, Anaheim

I respect Jim's heart and passion for helping students wrestle with critical issues. You will find *YouthBuilders* a great help in addressing themes which students face in everyday life.
Dann Spader, Executive Director, Sonlife Ministries

This new material by Jim Burns represents a vitality in curriculum and, I believe, a more mature and faithful direction. *YouthBuilders Group Bible Studies* challenges youth by teaching them how to make decisions rather than telling them what decisions to make. Each session offers teaching concepts, presents options and asks for a decision. I believe it's healthy, the way Christ taught and represents the abilities, personhood and faithfulness of youth. I give it an A+!
J. David Stone, President, Stone & Associates

YouthBuilders Group Bible Studies is a tremendous new set of resources for reaching students. Jim has his finger on the pulse of youth today. He understands their mind-sets, and has prepared these studies in a way that will capture their attention and lead to greater maturity in Christ. I heartily recommend these studies.
Rick Warren, Senior Pastor, Saddleback Valley Community Church

DEDICATION

To Jill Corey

YOUR PARTNERSHIP IN OUR MINISTRY IS...
YOUR COMMITMENT TO THIS CAUSE IS...
YOUR SELFLESSNESS AND DEDICATION IS...
YOUR LONGTIME FRIENDSHIP IS...

INCREDIBLE.

You are truly an incredible and remarkable person. Thank you for your years of support and leadership.
You are loved and appreciated.

Love in Christ,
Jim

C ONTENTS

THANKS AND THANKS AGAIN!

This project is definitely a team effort. First of all, thank you to Cathy, Christy, Rebecca and Heidi Burns, the women of my life.

Thank you to Jill Corey, my incredible assistant and longtime friend.

Thank you to Doug Webster for your outstanding job as executive director of the National Institute of Youth Ministry (NIYM).

Thank you to the NIYM staff in San Clemente: Teresa Parsons, Gary Lenhart, Roger Royster, Ron Spence, Luchi Bierbower, Dean Bruns, Laurie Pilz, Ken Bayard, Russ Cline and Larry Acosta.

Thank you to our 150-plus associate trainers who have been my coworkers, friends and sacrificial guinea pigs.

Thank you to Kyle Duncan, Bill Greig III and Jean Daly for convincing me that Gospel Light is a great publisher who deeply believes in the mission to reach young people. I believe!

Thank you to the Youth Specialties world. Tic, Mike and Wayne, so many years ago, you brought on a wet-behind-the-ears youth worker with hair and taught me most everything I know about youth work today.

Thank you to the hundreds of donors, supporters and friends of NIYM. You are helping create an international grassroots movement that is helping young people make positive decisions that will affect them for the rest of their lives.

"When there is no counsel, the people fall; But in the multitude of counselors there is safety" (Proverbs 11:14, *NKJV*).

Jim Burns
San Clemente, CA

YouthBuilders Group Bible Studies

It's Relational—Students learn best when they talk—not when you talk. There is always a get acquainted section in the Warm Up. All the experiences are based on building community in your group.

It's Biblical—With no apologies, this series in unashamedly Christian. Every session has a practical, relevant Bible study.

It's Experiential—Studies show that young people retain up to 85 percent of the material when they are *involved* in action-oriented, experiential learning. The sessions use role plays, discussion starters, case studies, graphs and other experiential, educational methods. *We believe it's a sin to bore a young person with the gospel.*

It's Interactive—This study is geared to get students feeling comfortable with sharing ideas and interacting with peers and leaders.

It's Easy to Follow—The sessions have been prepared by Jim Burns to allow the leader to pick up the material and use it. There is little preparation time on your part. Jim did the work for you.

It's Adaptable—You can pick and choose from several topics or go straight through the material as a whole study.

It's Age Appropriate—In the "Team Effort" section, one group experience relates best to junior high students while the other works better with high school students. Look at both to determine which option is best for your group.

It's Parent Oriented—The Parent Page helps you to do youth ministry at its finest. Christian education should take place in the home as well as in the church. The Parent Page is your chance to come alongside the parents and help them have a good discussion with their kids.

It's Proven—This material was not written by someone in an ivory tower. It was written for young people and has already been used with them. They love it.

How to Use This Study

The 12 sessions are divided into three stand-alone units. Each unit has four sessions. You may choose to teach all 12 sessions consecutively. Or you may use only one unit. Or you may present individual sessions. You know your group best so you choose.

Each of the 12 sessions is divided into five sections.

Warm Up—Young people will stay in your youth group if they feel comfortable and make friends in the group. This section is designed for you and the students to get to know each other better. These activities are filled with history-giving and affirming questions and experiences.

Team Effort—Following the model of Jesus, the Master Teacher, these activities engage young people in the session. Stories, group situations, surveys and more bring the session to the students. There is an option for junior high/middle school students and one for high school students.

In the Word—Most young people are biblically illiterate. These Bible studies present the Word of God and encourage students to see the relevance of the Scriptures to their lives.

Things to Think About—Young people need the opportunity to really think through the issues at hand. These discussion starters get students talking about the subject and interacting on important issues.

Parent Page—A youth worker can only do so much. Reproduce this page and get it into the hands of parents. This tool allows quality parent/teen communication that really brings the session home.

THE BIBLE TUCK-IN™

It's a tear-out sheet you fold and place in your Bible, containing the essentials you'll need for teaching your group.

HERE'S HOW TO USE IT:

To prepare for the session, first study the session. Tear out the Bible *Tuck-In*™ and personalize it by making notes. Fold the Bible *Tuck-In*™ in half on the dotted line. Slip it into your Bible for easy reference throughout the session. The Key Verse, Biblical Basis and Big Idea at the beginning of the Bible *Tuck-In*™ will help you keep the session on track. With the Bible *Tuck-In*™ your students will see that your teaching comes from the Bible and won't be distracted by a leader's guide.

GOD'S LOVE

LEADER'S PEP TALK

A few weeks ago I was speaking at a large youth gathering on the East Coast. I was intimidated by the size of this huge event and the talent of speakers and musicians. As I began to speak to the students about the *insanely generous gift of God's love,* I apologized for such a simple message.

A close friend of mine came up to me after a very inspiring response and said, "Great presentation; however, I have a bone to pick with you."

I sheepishly answered, "Okay, let 'er rip."

"You apologized for giving a simple gospel presentation on the love of God." He went on to confront me, "The love of God is the simplest message of all and the deepest at the same time. Judging from the response of this crowd of kids, they needed to be reminded that God loves them unconditionally." He ended, "Please don't ever apologize for the beauty of the gospel."

He was right. My apology was more to my communicator peers than to the kids. I realized that my friend was right, there is absolutely nothing more important or exciting, whether we hear it for the first time or one-thousandth time, than:

> For God so loved the world that he gave his one
> and only Son, that whoever believes in him shall
> not perish but have eternal life (John 3:16).

In this section you have the incredible opportunity to give your students the basics of the faith. What a joy and a privilege to present eternal basic truths to students. Some of your students will get it for the first time. For others it will be a review, but what a great and important review. Maybe these are the types of sessions we should present to our students more often. Putting the experiential learning pieces together for you from my work with students has brought me a whole new appreciation for the basics of Christianity.

I am reminded that as a Christian I am to love God, not out of responsibility and works, but simply out of a response for what He has done for me. After all, His reason for coming to the planet Earth was redemption. He has given us eternal life and an abundant life. Maybe that great theologian Vince Lombardi was right when he said,

"When you stray away from the basics you've gone a long way towards defeat."

If you can place these beautiful timeless principles of basic Christianity into the lives of your students you have given them the most important treasure available. Let's pray that God works wonders as you faithfully share His eternal truths with your students.

GOD'S UNCONDITIONAL LOVE

EY VERSE

"**B**ut we had to celebrate and be glad, because this brother of yours was dead and is alive again; he was lost and is found." Luke 15:32

IBLICAL BASIS

Luke 15:7,10-32;
Romans 5:8

HE BIG IDEA

God loves you unconditionally, not for what you do but for who you are—His child.

IMS OF THIS SESSION

During this session you will guide students to:

- Examine the depth of love God has for humankind;
- Discover how God's unconditional love relates to their lives;
- Implement a positive response of faith to God's never-ending love.

ARM UP

Introductions—

Students introduce each other and God.

TEAM EFFORT— JUNIOR HIGH/ MIDDLE SCHOOL

Prodigals—

A unique look at the story of the prodigal son.

TEAM EFFORT— HIGH SCHOOL

Loving the Unlovely—

A story displaying love when it is undeserved.

IN THE WORD

The Father's Love—

A Bible study on the love God has for His children.

THINGS TO THINK ABOUT (OPTIONAL)

Questions to get students thinking and talking about God's unconditional love.

PARENT PAGE

A tool to get the session into the home and allow parents and young people to discuss where they are in their relationships with God.

LEADER'S DEVOTIONAL

"But God demonstrates his own love for us in this: While we were still sinners, Christ died for us."—Romans 5:8

Do you remember when you used to play games as a kid and everyone would cry out, "Me first! Me first!" It didn't matter if it was playing baseball, breaking a piñata at a birthday party or running to the drinking fountain after a long, hot game of kickball. Almost everyone had a "me first" attitude.

As adults, some things never change. The "me first" or "who's best" attitudes are used by many adults to measure who has the biggest house, the nicest car or who took the most exotic vacation. It's called the Comparison Game. It's a game that no one wins and everyone loses. *Either I'm better than you or you're better than me and it all depends on how much stuff we each have.* That's the "me first" attitude in operation. It's a self-centered attitude that doesn't have youth ministry very high on the priority list. Why? Giving and serving teenagers challenges the "me first" attitude by honoring young people and serving their needs.

God has always had a "you first" attitude. The cornerstone of the Christian faith is found in God's giving, sacrificial and unconditional love for you. First John 4:19 says that we love God because He first loved us. God placed you and me before Himself. Jesus Christ gave up His life that we might have life in Him.

When was the last time you reminded yourself of God's unconditional love for you? Too often, youth workers focus on telling young people about God's unconditional love, but in the progress, forget to remind themselves of God's enduring love for them. This is a lesson to not only remind yourself of God's unconditional love for you, but to experience it as well. God wants His unconditional love to not only transform teenagers, but your life as well. (Written by Joey O'Connor.)

SESSION ONE   BIBLE TUCK-IN ™

GOD'S UNCONDITIONAL LOVE

KEY VERSE

"But we had to celebrate and be glad, because this brother of yours was dead and is alive again; he was lost and is found." Luke 15:32

BIBLICAL BASIS

Luke 15:7,10-32; Romans 5:8

THE BIG IDEA

God loves you unconditionally, not for what you do but for who you are—His child.

WARM UP (5-10 MINUTES)

INTRODUCTIONS

• Divide students into pairs.
• Have each student give his or her entire life story in one minute.
• Have the partners introduce each other to the whole group.
• Then give the pairs three minutes to come up with a paragraph on how they would introduce God to the group.
• Have some pairs share their introduction of God.

TEAM EFFORT—JUNIOR HIGH/MIDDLE SCHOOL (15-20 MINUTES)

PRODIGALS

• Give each student a copy of "Prodigals" on page 23 and a pen or pencil, or display a copy using an overhead projector.
• Read aloud the stories.
• Complete the page as a whole group.

Valley Girl Version

So like there was this old dude who had two sons. The youngest one was like y' know a total babe, for sure. The older one was a total zod, like a real space cadet, totally. So this young dude is like freakin' out, like totally bored and stiff. There was nothing to do, like nothing.

So he goes to his dad and says, "I'm sure I'm going to stay here for the rest of my life. Like gag me with a spoon. I mean barf me out. This place is totally gross, like grody to the max. I want like my share of your megabucks so I can pig out on junk food and buy clothes, for sure."

So his Dad like gave him his share of the megabucks and like this young babe went totally spaz, for sure, like scarf and junk food and lowlies to the max. And rolfing all night long. Like totally freaked me out. I am so sure. Gag me.

The Prodigal Son in F

Feeling footloose and frisky, a feather-brained fellow forced his found father to fork over the farthings. He flew far to foreign

21

Fold

THE MESSAGE

How does verse 32 summarize the entire parable?

(God rejoices when His children return to Him.)

THE PARABLE AND YOU

Room for Me

There are three main characters in the parable: the father, the younger son and his older brother. In the space below, list the character that best describes how you feel about your relationship with God and explain why.

....

Room to Grow

1. Why do many people desire to set out to do it their way?
2. When can this be good and when can this be harmful? Give examples. ....

Room for Rent

List any areas of your life in which you have strayed away from your heavenly Father in order to do your own thing. Then, circle those that need immediate attention. ....

Room for Free

1. How does it feel knowing that your heavenly Father, like the father in this story, has paid the price for your sin and celebrates when His children return to Him? ....

2. Read Romans 5:8. How does this verse relate to this story?

(God loves us no matter what our state or circumstance is.)

SO WHAT?

No matter what you do or don't do, God loves you! The love you receive from family or friends can change. God's love for you always remains the same because God doesn't change.

While we may know this, we may not always experience it. Pray now that God would make His love for you known to your mind and experienced by your heart.

THINGS TO THINK ABOUT (OPTIONAL)

• Use the questions on page 33 after or as a part of "In the Word."
1. Why is it often difficult to receive unconditional love from God or even others?

....

2. What makes the concept of God loving us unconditionally so inviting?

....

3. How would you describe God's love to someone who had never heard about it before?

....

PARENT PAGE

• Distribute page to parents.

fields and frittered his fortune, feasting fabulously with faithless friends. Finally facing famine and fleeced by his fellows-in-folly, he found himself a feed flinger in a filthy farmyard. Fairly famishing, he fain would have filled his frame with foraged food from the fodder fragments. "Phooey, my father's flunkies fare far fancier," the frazzled fugitive fumed feverishly, frankly facing facts. Frustrated by failure and filled with foreboding, he fled forthwith to his family. Falling at his father's feet, he floundered forlornly, "Father, I have flunked and fruitlessly forfeited family favor...." But the faithful father, fore-stalling further flinching, frantically flagged the flunkies to fetch forth the finest fatling and fix a feast.

The fugitive's fault-finding frater frowned on the fickle forgiveness of former folderol. His fury flashed—but hissing was futile. The farsighted father figured, "Such filial fidelity is fine, but what forbids fervent festivity—for the fugitive is found! Unfurl the flags! Former failure is forgotten, folly forsaken. Forgiveness forms the foundation for future fortitude."

Can you think of any other versions of this story? (Example, surf talk, cowboy, rap, etc.) If so, ask for ideas and create a new version or invite someone to write another version to share next session.

Why do you think the prodigal son parable is one of Jesus' most well-known parables?

....

What does this parable tell us about God?

....

 *T*EAM EFFORT—HIGH SCHOOL (15-20 MINUTES)

LOVING THE UNLOVELY

• Display a copy of "Loving the Unlovely" on page 25 using an overhead projector.
• Read aloud the story.
• Students respond to questions as a whole group.

Once upon a time there was a young girl named Susie. She was a beautiful little girl with the most wonderful doll collection in the world. Her father traveled all over the world on business, and for nearly 12 years he had brought dolls home to Susie. In her bedroom she had shelves of dolls from all over the United States and from every other continent on Earth. She had dolls that could sing and dance and do just about anything a doll could possibly do.

One day her father's business acquaintances came to visit. At dinner he asked Susie about her wonderful doll collection. After dinner Susie took him by the hand and showed him these marvelous dolls from all over the world. He was very impressed. After he took the grand tour and was introduced to many of the beautiful dolls, he asked Susie, "With all these precious dolls you must have one that is your favorite. Which one is it?"

Without a moment's hesitation Susie went over to her old beat-up toy box and started pulling out toys. From the bottom of the box she pulled out one of the most ragged dolls you have ever seen. There were only a few strands of hair left on the head. The clothing had long since disappeared. The doll was filthy from many years of play outside. One of the buttons for the eyes was hanging down with only string to keep it connected. Stuffing was coming out at the elbow and knee. Susie handed the doll to the gentleman and said, "This doll is my favorite."

The man was shocked and asked, "Why this doll with all these beautiful dolls in your room?"

She replied, "If I didn't love this doll nobody would!"

That single statement moved the businessman to tears. It was such a simple statement, yet so profound. The little girl loved her doll unconditionally. She loved the doll not for its beauty or abilities but simply because it was her very own doll.

1. How do you think this story could apply to the love God has for you?

-------- Fold --------

2. Are there any stories in the Bible that remind you of the story?

....

3. Why do many people have a hard time accepting God's unconditional love in their lives?

....

*I*N THE WORD (25-30 MINUTES)

THE FATHER'S LOVE

• Divide students into groups of three or four.
• Give each student a copy of "The Father's Love" on pages 27 to 31 and a pen or pencil, or display a copy using an overhead projector.
• Students complete the Bible study.
• Read Luke 15:11-32.

THE SON

1. What did the younger son request from his father?
(His share of his father's estate.)

2. What did the son do after he received his request?
(He left his home and spent his money.)

3. In the far country this Jewish son worked on a pig farm (see verses 15,16). The Jews follow the Old Testament Law and do not eat pork; pigs are listed in the Law as an unclean animal. Knowing this, what is the significance of the son's occupation?
(He took one of the most degrading jobs possible.)

4. What was the result of the son's choices and actions?
(He was left without anything: family, home, money.)

THE FATHER

1. How did the father respond to the son's coming home? Was this the expected response?
(He ran out to meet his son which the son didn't expect.)

2. According to Luke 15:7,10, how does God respond to the homecoming of a lost sinner?
(God rejoices.)

THE OLDER BROTHER

1. Why do you think the older brother reacted the way he did?
(He was jealous.)

2. What was the father's response to the older brother?
(He explains the special circumstances of the younger son and reassures the older son of his love for him.)

3. According to Luke 15:7,10, how does God respond to the homecoming of a lost sinner?
(God rejoices.)

TEAM EFFORT

PRODIGALS

Valley Girl Version[1]

So like there was this old dude who had two sons. The youngest one was like y' know a total babe, for sure. The older one was a total zod, like a real space cadet, totally. So this young dude is like freakin' out, like totally bored and stiff. There was nothing to do, like nothing.

So he goes to his dad and says, "I'm sure I'm going to stay here for the rest of my life. Like gag me with a spoon. I mean barf me out. This place is totally gross, like grody to the max. I want like my share of your megabucks so I can pig out on junk food and buy clothes, for sure."

So his Dad like gave him his share of the megabucks and like this young babe went totally spaz. For sure, like scarf and junk food and lowies to the max. And rolfing all night long. Like totally freaked me out. I am so sure. Gag me.

The Prodigal Son in F[2]

Feeling footloose and frisky, a feather-brained fellow forced his found father to fork over the farthings. He flew far to foreign fields and frittered his fortune, feasting fabulously with faithless friends. Finally facing famine and fleeced by his fellows-in-folly, he found himself a feed flinger in a filthy farmyard. Fairly famishing, he fain would have filled his frame with foraged food from the fodder fragments. "Phooey, my father's flunkies fare far fancier," the frazzled fugitive fumed feverishly, frankly facing facts. Frustrated by failure and filled with foreboding, he fled forthwith to his family. Falling at his father's feet, he floundered forlornly, "Father, I have flunked and fruitlessly forfeited family favor...." But the faithful father, forestalling further flinching, frantically flagged the flunkies to fetch forth the finest fatling and fix a feast.

The fugitive's fault-finding frater frowned on the fickle forgiveness of former folderol. His fury flashed—but fussing was futile. The farsighted father figured, "Such filial fidelity is fine, but what forbids fervent festivity—for the fugitive is found! Unfurl the flags! Former failure is forgotten, folly forsaken. Forgiveness forms the foundation for future fortitude."

1. Can you think of any other versions of this story? (Example, surf talk, cowboy, rap, etc.) If so, create a new version now or write another version to share next session.

....

....

2. Why do you think the prodigal son parable is one of Jesus's most well-known parables?

....

....

3. What does this parable tell us about God?

....

....

Note

1. Bill Patterson, *Ideas 25-28* (Grand Rapids, MI: Zondervan, 1985). Used by permission.

2. Wayne Rice and Mike Yaconelli, *Greatest Skits on Earth, Volume 2* (Grand Rapids, MI: Zondervan, 1987). Used by permission.

TEAM EFFORT

LOVING THE UNLOVELY

Once upon a time there was a young girl named Susie. She was a beautiful little girl with the most wonderful doll collection in the world. Her father traveled all over the world on business, and for nearly 12 years he had brought dolls home to Susie. In her bedroom she had shelves of dolls from all over the United States and from every other continent on Earth. She had dolls that could sing and dance and do just about anything a doll could possibly do.

One day one of her father's business acquaintances came to visit. At dinner he asked Susie about her wonderful doll collection. After dinner Susie took him by the hand and showed him these marvelous dolls from all over the world. He was very impressed. After he took the grand tour and was introduced to many of the beautiful dolls, he asked Susie, "With all these precious dolls you must have one that is your favorite. Which one is it?" Without a moment's hesitation Susie went over to her old beat-up toy box and started pulling out toys. From the bottom of the box she pulled out one of the most ragged dolls you have ever seen. There were only a few strands of hair left on the head. The clothing had long since disappeared. The doll was filthy from many years of play outside. One of the buttons for the eyes was hanging down with only string to keep it connected. Stuffing was coming out at the elbow and knee. Susie handed the doll to the gentleman and said, "This doll is my favorite."

The man was shocked and asked, "Why this doll with all these beautiful dolls in your room?"

She replied, "If I didn't love this doll nobody would!"

That single statement moved the businessman to tears. It was such a simple statement, yet so profound. The little girl loved her doll unconditionally. She loved the doll not for its beauty or abilities but simply because it was her very own doll.

1. How do you think this story could apply to the love God has for you?

....

....

2. Are there any stories in the Bible that remind you of the story?

....

....

3. Why do many people have a hard time accepting God's unconditional love in their lives?

....

....

....

IN THE WORD

THE FATHER'S LOVE

Jesus continued: "There was a man who had two sons. The younger one said to his father, 'Father, give me my share of the estate.' So he divided his property between them.

"Not long after that, the younger son got together all he had, set off for a distant country and there squandered his wealth in wild living. After he had spent everything, there was a severe famine in that whole country, and he began to be in need. So he went and hired himself out to a citizen of that country, who sent him to his fields to feed pigs. He longed to fill his stomach with the pods that the pigs were eating, but no one gave him anything.

"When he came to his senses, he said, 'How many of my father's hired men have food to spare, and here I am starving to death! I will set out and go back to my father and say to him: Father, I have sinned against heaven and against you. I am no longer worthy to be called your son; make me like one of your hired men.' So he got up and went to his father.

"But while he was still a long way off, his father saw him and was filled with compassion for him; he ran to his son, threw his arms around him and kissed him.

"The son said to him, 'Father, I have sinned against heaven and you. I am no longer worthy to be called your son.'

"But the father said to his servants, 'Quick! Bring the best robe and put it on him. Put a ring on his finger and sandals on his feet. Bring the fattened calf and kill it. Let's have a feast and celebrate. For this son of mine was dead and is alive again; he was lost and is found.' So they began to celebrate.

"Meanwhile, the older son was in the field. When he came near the house, he heard music and dancing. So he called one of the servants and asked him what was going on. 'Your brother has come,' he replied, 'and your father has killed the fattened calf because he has him back safe and sound.'

"The older brother became angry and refused to go in. So his father went out and pleaded with him. But he answered his father, 'Look! All these years I've been slaving for you and never disobeyed your orders. Yet you never gave me even a young goat so I could celebrate with my friends. But when this son of yours who has squandered your property with prostitutes comes home, you kill the fattened calf for him!'

"'My son,' the father said, 'you are always with me, and everything I have is yours. But we had to celebrate and be glad, because this brother of yours was dead and is alive again; he was lost and is found'" (Luke 15:11-32).

The Son

1. What did the younger son request from his father?

....

....

2. What did the son do after he received his request?

....

....

IN THE WORD

3. In the far country this Jewish son worked on a pig farm (see verses 15,16). The Jews follow the Old Testament Law and do not eat pork; pigs are listed in the Law as an unclean animal. Knowing this, what is the significance of the son's occupation?

....

....

4. What was the result of the son's choices and actions?

....

....

The Father

1. How did the father respond to the son's coming home? Was this the expected response?

....

....

2. According to Luke 15:7,10, how does God respond to the homecoming of a lost sinner?

....

....

The Older Brother

1. Why do you think the older brother reacted the way he did?

....

....

2. What was the father's response to the older brother?

....

....

The Message

How does verse 32 summarize the entire parable?

....

....

IN THE WORD

The Parable and You
Room for Me
There are three main characters in the parable: the father, the younger son and his older brother. In the space below, list the character that best describes how you feel about your relationship with God and explain why.

....
....
....

Room to Grow

1. Why do many people desire to set out to do it their way?

....
....

2. When can this be good and when can this be harmful? Give examples.

....
....

Room for Rent
List any areas of your life in which you have strayed away from your heavenly Father in order to do your own thing. Then, circle those that need immediate attention.

....
....

Room for Free

1. How does it feel knowing that your heavenly Father, like the father in this story, has paid the price for your sin and celebrates when His children return to Him?

....
....

2. Read Romans 5:8. How does this verse relate to this story?

....
....
....

SO WHAT?

No matter what you do or don't do, God loves you! The love you receive from family or friends can change. God's love for you always remains the same because God doesn't change.

While we may know this, we may not always experience it. Pray now that God would make His love for you known to your mind and experienced by your heart.

*T*HINGS TO THINK ABOUT

1. Why is it often difficult to receive unconditional love from God or even others?

....
....
....

2. What makes the concept of God loving us unconditionally so inviting?

....
....
....

3. How would you describe God's love to someone who had never heard about it before?

....
....
....

PARENT PAGE

Read Luke 15:11-32.

Mark an *X* on the story line that best describes your place on the journey with God.

Living as a part of God's family

Criticizing the Father's actions

Heading out to do it my way

Loving welcome from the Father

Hard times and pig sties

Deciding to head home to the Father

President Abraham Lincoln was asked how he was going to treat the rebellious Southerners when they had finally been defeated and had returned to the Union of the United States. Lincoln answered, "I'll treat them as if they had never been away."[1]

1. How is Abe Lincoln's attitude similar to the father's in the parable?

....

....

....

2. What is your response to your Father who always welcomes you home?

....

....

....

Note

1. William Barclay, *The Gospel of Luke: The Daily Bible Study Series* (Philadelphia, PA: Westminster Press, 1975), p. 205.

Session 1 "God's Unconditional Love" Date ....

NEW LIFE

KEY VERSE

"For God so loved the world that he gave his one and only Son, that whoever believes in him shall not perish but have eternal life."
John 3:16

BIBLICAL BASIS

Proverbs 14:12;
Isaiah 59:2;
John 1:12; 3:1-21; 10:10; 19:39;
Romans 3:23; 5:1,8; 6:23; 10:9;
1 Timothy 2:5;
1 Peter 3:18;
1 John 1:9;
Revelation 3:20

THE BIG IDEA

Because Jesus Christ died for our sins, we can have a brand-new life and relationship with God.

AIMS OF THIS SESSION

During this session you will guide students to:
• Examine what the Bible has to say about a new relationship with God;
• Discover the biblical principles for being spiritually born again;
• Implement a decision to either renew or begin a new life with God.

WARM UP

Dudley DoRight—
A classic melodrama.

TEAM EFFORT— JUNIOR HIGH/ MIDDLE SCHOOL

A Starting-over Ceremony—
Students express their desire to begin anew with God.

TEAM EFFORT— HIGH SCHOOL
Nailing Our Sins to the Cross—
A graphic expression of a new beginning with God.

IN THE WORD

A New Life—
A Bible study on the new life Jesus brings.

THINGS TO THINK ABOUT(OPTIONAL)

Questions to get students thinking and talking about new life in Jesus.

PARENT PAGE

A tool to get the session into the home and allow parents and young people to discuss the process of beginning anew with God.

LEADER'S DEVOTIONAL

"Her papery skin a ghostly, grayish white, her gums bleeding and her heartbeat irregular, Christy Henrich withered to little more than a skeleton. She was engaged to be married and still hadn't reached puberty at 22, her emaciated body tricked her into perpetual childhood by a self-inflicted starvation diet that led her to death two weeks ago."—San Diego Union-Tribune, August 9, 1994

In a nation full of food, it's difficult to imagine a person starving herself to death. Christy Henrich, the Olympic gymnast, died of "multiple organ system failure" after a decade-long, intense struggle with anorexia and bulimia. Her tragic death is the sad consequence of a ruthless eating disorder that literally devours its victims. Couldn't the same tragedy be said of the millions of people whose hearts and souls are starving for new life in Christ?

New life in Jesus Christ is the solid answer to a starving world full of hungry hearts. Though Christy Henrich refused to eat the food that provided health and life to her body, it's clear that her hunger went beyond the four basic food groups. She was starving for love. For a sense of belonging. Significance. Esteem. Attention. She was starving for everything that Jesus freely gives in His love and compassion for us. Though her family members desperately tried to help her, Christy's disease distorted and warped her perception of herself and those closest to her.

What part of your heart is starving for attention? What needs in your life are screaming out in hunger? What are you looking for to satisfy you like nothing else? Just as the students in your youth ministry have special needs, wants and desires, it's critical to examine your own needs, wants and desires.

Everything that you and I could possibly hope for is found in Christ Jesus. He is the only one who can truly satisfy all of our needs. Material possessions, professional status, relationships, fame or fortune can never give us the truly deep and satisfying quality of life we desire. Only Jesus Christ, through the power of the Holy Spirit, can calm our restless, hungry hearts. Our souls can rest in Him. Full. Content. Satisfied. This week, remember the wonderful words of Jesus. "I am the bread of life. He who comes to me will never go hungry, and he who believes in me will never be thirsty" (John 6:35). (Written by Joey O'Connor.)

S E S S I O N   T W O

NEW LIFE

KEY VERSE

"For God so loved the world that he gave his one and only Son, that whoever believes in him shall not perish but have eternal life." John 3:16

BIBLICAL BASIS

Proverbs 14:12; Isaiah 59:2; John 1:12; 3:1-21; 10:10; 19:39; Romans 3:23; 5:1,8; 6:23; 10:9; 1 Timothy 2:5; 1 Peter 3:18; 1 John 1:9; Revelation 3:20

THE BIG IDEA

Because Jesus Christ died for our sins, we can have a brand-new life and relationship with God.

WARM UP (10-15 MINUTES)

DUDLEY DORIGHT

• Assign melodrama roles.
• Give each character a copy of "Dudley DoRight" on page 41.
• As the narrator reads melodrama, characters perform actions.
• The characters:

1. The hero, Dudley DoRight
2. The heroine, Prudence PureHeart
3. The villain, Dirty Dan
4. Grandmother
5. Dog (a boy who gets down on all fours)
6. Cat (a girl who does the same)
7. Chair (a boy on his hands and knees)
8. Table (two boys, side by side on their hands and knees)
9. Narrator

TEAM EFFORT—JUNIOR HIGH/MIDDLE SCHOOL (15-20 MINUTES)

A STARTING-OVER CEREMONY

• Give each student a piece of paper and pen or pencil.
• Have students write two to five areas of their lives that they would like to give to Christ and start over.
• Read aloud John 3:16 and then discuss these questions:

How does this verse relate to starting over?

Fold

What makes this story so meaningful?

SO WHAT?

Place a mark next to the phrase below that best describes your response to the eternal message of Jesus: "You must be born again" (John 3:7).

☐ I have experienced new birth in my life.
☐ I'm not interested in experiencing new birth at this time.
☐ It sounds interesting but I really don't understand the concept of new birth. (If you have questions, this message is too important for you not to talk with someone about it!)
☐ I'm interested in experiencing new birth at this time. (You can pray the following prayer to express this desire:)

Dear Lord Jesus,
I know that I am a sinner and need Your forgiveness. I believe that You died for my sins. I now want to turn from my sins. I now invite You to come into my heart and life. I want to trust and follow You as Lord and Savior. In Jesus' name. Amen.

THINGS TO THINK ABOUT (OPTIONAL)

• Use the questions on page 49 after or as a part of "In the Word."
1. What does "new life in Christ" mean to you?

2. What holds people back from starting over with God?

3. What steps of faith do you need to take right now?

PARENT PAGE

• Distribute page to parents.

What hope does this statement give us?

How is God's love expressed in this verse?

TEAM EFFORT—HIGH SCHOOL (15-20 MINUTES)

NAILING OUR SINS TO THE CROSS

- Have a large wooden cross, nails, a couple of hammers, a tape recorder or CD player and soft, reflective music.
- Give each student a piece of paper and pen or pencil.
- Have students write down the sins that come to mind on the paper.
- Read aloud John 3:16 and 1 John 1:9.
- Have the students literally nail their sins on the wooden cross as students are quiet and music is playing.
- Pray, emphasizing God's forgiveness and the assurance of a new life in Christ.
- Take the sins off the cross and destroy the pieces of paper.

IN THE WORD (20-25 MINUTES)

A NEW LIFE

- Divide students into pairs.
- Give each student a copy of "A New Life" on pages 43 and 45 and a pen or pencil, or display a copy using an overhead projector.
- Students complete the Bible study.

Read John 3:1-21.

You've just read one of the most powerful and important conversations ever recorded in the life of Jesus. For the most part, Jesus was surrounded by the ordinary people of His day. However, in this conversation we see Him with one of the most important Jewish leaders of His time.

We know Nicodemus was a rich man. When Jesus died, Nicodemus brought a "mixture of myrrh and aloes, about seventy-five pounds" (John 19:39) for Jesus' body. Only a wealthy man could afford such a gift.

Nicodemus was a Pharisee, and in many ways the Pharisees were the most important people in the whole country of Israel. There were never more than 6,000 at a time, and they all were completely dedicated to observing every detail of the Old Testament Law. Nicodemus was a member of the Sanhedrin which was composed of 70 religious leaders. The Sanhedrin was the supreme court of the Jewish people.

What is the significance of an important man like Nicodemus talking with Jesus about being born again?

Why do you suppose Nicodemus came to Jesus at night?

What is the main theme of this conversation?

This conversation between Jesus and Nicodemus is often confusing to many people. List below any questions you may have about this conversation.

I. You can be spiritually born again.
A. If Jesus came to you and declared, "I tell you the truth, no one can see the kingdom of God unless he is born again" (John 3:3), how would you respond?

B. To be "born again" literally means to be born spiritually from above. What great message of hope do you see in this passage?

II. New life begins with God's love.
A. How does John 3:16 validate the above statement?

III. You can be assured of your new life in Christ.
How does this passage give you the assurance of your salvation in Christ? (See John 3:1-8, 16.)

B. According to verse 16, do you agree with the statement, "The mainspring of God's being is love"? (Please write yes or no and why.)

Here is a great story:

A recent convert to Jesus was approached by an unbelieving friend: "So you have been converted to Christ?"
"Yes."
"Then you must know a great deal about Him. Tell me, what country was He born in?"
"I don't know."
"What was His age when He died?"
"I don't know."
"How many sermons did He preach?"
"I don't know."
"You certainly know very little for a man who claims to be converted to Christ."
"You are right. I am ashamed of how little I know about Him. But this much I know: Three years ago I was a drunkard; I was in debt; my family was falling to pieces and they dreaded the sight of me. But now I have given up drinking. We are out of debt. Ours is a happy home. My children eagerly await my return home each evening. All this Christ has done for me. This much I know of Christ!"

WARM UP

DUDLEY DORIGHT[1]

• The characters:

1. The hero, Dudley DoRight
2. The heroine, Prudence PureHeart
3. The villain, Dirty Dan
4. Grandmother
5. Dog (a boy who gets down on all fours)
6. Cat (a girl who does the same)
7. Chair (a boy on his hands and knees)
8. Table (two boys, side by side on their hands and knees)
9. Narrator

As our story opens, we find ourselves in a densely wooded forest where lovely Prudence PureHeart is picking wild blackberries while whistling a merry tune. (Pause while Prudence whistles, etc.) Unbeknownst to her, the village villain, Dirty Dan, is creeping up behind her. He grabs her and tries to steal a kiss! She screams loud and long. The villain covers her mouth with his hand as she screams. She slaps the villain in the face. He picks her up over his shoulder and carries her. She screams and beats him. He marches around in a circle three times, then heads for home to steal her grandmother's money. They exit.

Meanwhile back at the ranch, Prudence's grandmother is sitting on a chair stirring some cake batter on the table. The cat is sleeping underneath the table. The old dog, Shep, enters the house and barks at the cat. The cat jumps into Grandma's lap. Grandmother slaps the cat and says, "Get down, you dirty creature." The cat jumps down and runs outside. The dog comes over and licks Grandma's hand. He keeps licking her hand all the way up to the elbow. Grandma kicks the dog. The dog goes over and lies in the corner. Just then, the villain enters the room with Prudence on his shoulder. Grandmother screams. The villain says, "I am taking Prudence and your money." The dog rushes over and bites the villain on the leg. The villain kicks the dog and lets Prudence down. Prudence faints onto the floor. The dog barks at the villain, then goes over and starts licking Prudence's face to revive her. He licks her face for 15 seconds while she remains perfectly still.

Just then, our hero, Dudley DoRight, enters and shouts, "Forsooth and anon!" Prudence stands up and screams, "Oh, my darling Dudley!" Dudley and Prudence embrace. Dudley says, "I love you, my precious." Prudence says, "I love you, my little lotus blossom." All of a sudden the villain picks up the chair and throws it at Dudley. It knocks Dudley down to the floor. Prudence faints and falls onto the table. Grandmother tries to revive her by slapping her hand, while sobbing, "My child, my child." This goes on and on...

The cat re-enters the house, jumps on the chair and runs underneath the table. Dudley stands up and begins flexing his muscles. The villain begins to tremble and shake and his knees knock together. This goes on and on. The dog starts barking and the cat starts meowing and this goes on and on. Dudley decides to warm up for the fight so he does a few exercises by starting out with 10 jumping jacks. Then he runs in place for 15 seconds. While Grandmother is sobbing and slapping, the villain is trembling, the dog is barking and the cat is meowing. Then Dudley does 15 pushups. On the 15th pushup, the villain seizes his opportunity and hits Dudley on the head. Dudley falls to the floor, unconscious.

Just then the cat scratches the dog's nose. The dog and cat have a fight right on top of Dudley for 10 seconds. Then the dog chases the cat outside. Just then the table collapses under Prudence's weight and falls to the ground...table, Prudence, Grandmother and all. Prudence remains unconscious. Granny shouts, "You nasty villain!" and starts hitting him in the stomach. The villain doubles over. Granny then goes around and kicks him in the seat. The villain straightens up. She hits him some more in the stomach over and over. The villain again bends over. She gives him a rabbit punch on the back of the neck. He collapses unconscious to the floor. Granny looks around at the three unconscious bodies. She then straightens her shawl around her head and heads for the door for a night on the town saying, "All's well that ends well!"

Note

1. Larry Wiens, *Ideas 1-4* (El Cajon, CA: Youth Specialties, 1979), pp. 166-169. Used by permission.

 N THE WORD

A NEW LIFE

Read John 3:1-21.

You've just read one of the most powerful and important conversations ever recorded in the life of Jesus. For the most part, Jesus was surrounded by the ordinary people of His day. However, in this conversation we see Him with one of the important Jewish leaders of His time.

We know Nicodemus was a rich man. When Jesus died, Nicodemus brought a "mixture of myrrh and aloes, about seventy-five pounds" (John 19:39) for Jesus' body. Only a wealthy man could afford such a gift.

Nicodemus was a Pharisee, and in many ways the Pharisees were the most important people in the whole country of Israel. There were never more than 6,000 at a time and they all were completely dedicated to observing every detail of the Old Testament Law. Nicodemus was a member of the Sanhedrin which was composed of 70 religious leaders. The Sanhedrin was the supreme court of the Jewish people.

What is the significance of an important man like Nicodemus talking with Jesus about being born again?

....

....

....

Why do you suppose Nicodemus came to Jesus at night?

....

....

....

What is the main theme of this conversation?

....

....

....

This conversation between Jesus and Nicodemus is often confusing to many people. List below any questions you may have about this conversation.

....

....

....

....

....

IN THE WORD

I.   You can be spiritually born again.

   A.   If Jesus came to you and declared, "I tell you the truth, no one can see the kingdom of God unless he is born again" (John 3:3), how would you respond?

....

....

   B.   To be "born again" literally means to be born spiritually from above. What great message of hope do you see in this passage?

....

....

II.   New life begins with God's love.

   A.   How does John 3:16 validate the above statement?

....

....

   B.   According to verse 16, do you agree with the statement, "The mainspring of God's being is love"[1]? (Please write yes or no and why.)

....

....

III. You can be assured of your new life in Christ.

   How does this passage give you the assurance of your salvation in Christ? (See John 3:1-8,16.)

....

....

Here is a great story:

A recent convert to Jesus was approached by an unbelieving friend: "So you have been converted to Christ?"

"Yes."

"Then you must know a great deal about Him. Tell me, what country was He born in?"

"I don't know."

"What was His age when He died?"

"I don't know."

"How many sermons did He preach?"

"I don't know."

"You certainly know very little for a man who claims to be converted to Christ."

"You are right. I am ashamed of how little I know about Him. But this much I know: Three years ago I was a drunkard; I was in debt; my family was falling to pieces and they dreaded the sight of me. But now I have given up drinking. We are out of debt. Ours is a happy home. My children eagerly await my return home each evening. All this Christ has done for me. This much I know of Christ!"

What makes this story so meaningful?

....

....

....

....

....

....

Note

1. William Barclay, *The Gospel of John: The Daily Bible Study Series* (Philadelphia, PA: Westminster Press, 1975), p. 137.

So WHAT?

Place a mark next to the phrase below that best describes your response to the eternal message of Jesus: "You must be born again" (John 3:7).

- ☐ I have experienced new birth in my life.
- ☐ I'm not interested in experiencing new birth at this time.
- ☐ It sounds interesting but I really don't understand the concept of new birth. (If you have questions, this message is too important for you not to talk with someone about it!)
- ☐ I'm interested in experiencing new birth at this time. (You can pray the following prayer to express this desire:)
  Dear Lord Jesus,
  I know that I am a sinner and need Your forgiveness. I believe that You died for my sins. I want to turn from my sins. I now invite You to come into my heart and life. I want to trust and follow You as Lord and Savior.
  In Jesus' name. Amen.

THINGS TO THINK ABOUT

1. What does "new life in Christ" mean to you?

....
....
....

2. What holds people back from starting over with God?

....
....
....

3. What steps of faith do you need to take right now?

....
....
....

PARENT PAGE

STEPS TO PEACE WITH GOD

Read through this important process of new life written by the Billy Graham Association.

Step 1: God's Purpose: Peace and Life

God wants you to experience peace and life—abundant and eternal.

The Bible says...

"We have peace with God through our Lord Jesus Christ" (Romans 5:1).

"For God so loved the world that he gave his one and only Son, that whoever believes in him shall not perish but have eternal life" (John 3:16).

"I have come that they may have life, and have it to the full" (John 10:10).

Step 2: Our Problem: Separation

God created us in His own image to have an abundant life. He did not make us robots to automatically love and obey Him, but gave us a will and a freedom of choice.

We choose to disobey God and go our own willful way. We still make this choice today. This results in separation from God.

The Bible says...

"For all have sinned and fall short of the glory of God" (Romans 3:23).

"For the wages of sin is death, but the gift of God is eternal life in Christ Jesus our Lord" (Romans 6:23).

OUR ATTEMPTS:

Through the ages, individuals have tried in many ways to bridge the gap...without success...

The Bible says...

"There is a way that seems right to a man, but in the end it leads to death" (Proverbs 14:12).

"But your iniquities have separated you from your God; your sins have hidden his face from you, so that he will not hear" (Isaiah 59:2).

Step 3: God's Remedy: the Cross

Jesus Christ is the only answer to this problem. He died on the Cross and rose from the grave, paying the penalty for our sins and bridging the gap between God and people.

The Bible says...

"For there is one God and one mediator between God and men, the man Christ Jesus" (1 Timothy 2:5).

"For Christ died for sins once and for all, the righteous for the unrighteous, to bring you to God" (1 Peter 3:18).

"But God demonstrates His own love for us in this: While we were still sinners, Christ died for us" (Romans 5:8).

Step 4: Our Response: Receive Christ

We must trust Jesus Christ and receive Him by personal invitation.

The Bible says...

"Here I am! I stand at the door and knock. If anyone hears my voice and opens the door, I will come in and eat with him, and he with me" (Revelation 3:20).

"Yet to all who received him, to those who believed in his name, he gave the right to become children of God" (John 1:12).

"If you confess with your mouth, 'Jesus is Lord,' and believe in your heart that God raised him from the dead, you will be saved" (Romans 10:9).

RESPONSE:

Dear Lord Jesus,

I know that I am a sinner and need Your forgiveness. I believe that You died for my sins. I want to turn from my sins. I now invite You to come into my heart and life. I want to trust and follow You as Lord and Savior.

In Jesus' name. Amen.

Have you made this important decision at one time in your life?
☐ Yes   ☐ No   ☐ Not Sure

Do you have any questions?

....

....

....

If not, why not pray this prayer right now?

....

....

....

....

Session 2 "New Life" Date..................................

A LIFESTYLE OF LOVE

HELPS FOR SHARING YOUR FAITH

KEY VERSE

"The woman said, 'I know that Messiah' (called Christ) 'is coming. When he comes, he will explain everything to us.' Then Jesus declared, 'I who speak to you am he.'" John 4:25,26

BIBLICAL BASIS

Matthew 4:18-20;
John 4:4-26,39-42;
Acts 26

THE BIG IDEA

Our lives and actions are our greatest witness. You must earn the right to be heard, and then speak the truths of Jesus Christ.

AIMS OF THIS SESSION

During this session you will guide students to:
• Examine a biblical way of sharing their faith through their lifestyles;
• Discover practical ways to share their faith more effectively;
• Implement a specific plan to share their faith through lifestyles and witness.

WARM UP

God and You—
Students share their thoughts on their relationships with God.

TEAM EFFORT— JUNIOR HIGH/ MIDDLE SCHOOL

The Ragman—
A dramatic story of Christ's sacrifice for all.

TEAM EFFORT— HIGH SCHOOL

Meeting People's Needs—
An inventory of meeting people's needs with the gospel.

IN THE WORD

Sharing the Good News—
A Bible study and practical plan for sharing your faith.

THINGS TO THINK ABOUT (OPTIONAL)

Questions to get students thinking and talking about sharing their faith.

PARENT PAGE

A tool to get the session into the home and allow parents and young people to discuss how to be a witness.

LEADER'S DEVOTIONAL

"Let's believe in God's love, and let's be faithful to him. If you look at the cross, you will see his head lowered to kiss you. You will see his arms stretched out to embrace you. You will see his heart out to welcome you. Don't be afraid. He loves us, and he wants us to love one another."—Mother Teresa

Giving Jesus to others, especially young people, is something we should never be afraid or ashamed of. Sharing the gift of God's unconditional love is the most priceless, beautiful gift you could ever give someone. When you share the love of Jesus Christ, you are literally sharing the opportunity of new life. Putting God's love into action requires courage, gentleness and humility as you allow Christ to work through your life.

I love the bold, yet simple way Mother Teresa shares her love for Jesus Christ. She is a hero of the faith for her humble, childlike belief in God. Has Mother Teresa won the respect of millions for being a tremendous speaker? Did she win the Nobel Peace Prize for being young and creative? Have over 80,000 people joined her missionary order because she's a brilliant strategist? All these questions receive a resounding, "No!" Mother Teresa has won the hearts of millions of people because she has a simple devotion to the Lord as seen in her work with the poorest of the poor. St. Francis of Assisi once said, "Go into all the nations and make disciples of all men and if you must, use words." Our lives must come before our words.

Sharing a lifestyle of love first begins with your actions and then your words. People are looking for a demonstration of the gospel before an explanation of the gospel. When young people see the presence of Jesus Christ in your life, then your words will begin to make sense. God wants to use you in a simple way to make major changes in the lives of teenagers. It is your ears, hands, legs, mouth and heart that are His tools for His glory. You are an instrument of Jesus Christ, an ambassador for God and minister of reconciliation. Because of God's continual work in your life, people will have the impression that Jesus Christ has come into the world again. (Written by Joey O'Connor.)

A LIFESTYLE OF LOVE HELPS FOR SHARING YOUR FAITH

KEY VERSE

"The woman said, 'I know that Messiah' (called Christ) 'is coming. When he comes, he will explain everything to us.' Then Jesus declared, 'I who speak to you am he.'" John 4:25,26

BIBLICAL BASIS

Matthew 4:18-20; John 4:4-26,39-42; Acts 26

THE BIG IDEA

Our lives and actions are our greatest witness. You must earn the right to be heard, and then speak the truths of Jesus Christ.

WARM UP (5-10 MINUTES)

GOD AND YOU

- Divide students into groups of three or four.
- Give each student a copy of "God and You" on page 57 and a pen or pencil, or display a copy using an overhead projector.
- Students answer questions.

What is one of your first memories of hearing about God?

What people have been positive spiritual influences in your life?

When did God become real in your life? (If you aren't sure if He has, it's okay to share that.)

55

Fold

---

pointed her to her real need without condemning her. John 4:16-21 is a wonderful example of Jesus leading someone to the truth. He did it without condemning or without getting sidetracked with secondary issues. Summarize in your own words how Jesus led the conversation.

1. Why would condemning her not have helped His relationship with her?
(He wouldn't have had an opportunity to speak with her because she wouldn't have wanted to listen to someone who was condemning her.)

2. In this conversation (verses 16-21), she began to get sidetracked. How did Jesus lead her back to the central issue?
(He briefly answers her question and relates the answer back to her need for eternal life.)

3. What are some ways you can let people know you care for them even when you disapprove of their lifestyles?

D. Give people a positive encounter with the person of Jesus Christ.
Jesus confronted the woman with the fact that He was the Messiah. Now she must respond.

1. What are some ways you can help your friends and family have a positive encounter with the person of Jesus Christ?

2. What are the results shown in John 4:39-42 of Jesus' conversation with the Samaritan woman?

SO WHAT?

Now go back to your common interest/sharing your faith list and jot down the names of two people who you will actively pursue to love, minister and share your faith with.

Name	What you plan to do	When will you begin?

THINGS TO THINK ABOUT (OPTIONAL)

- Use the questions on page 75 after or as a part of "In the Word."

1. Why are some Christians afraid to share their faith?

2. What attracted you to Christianity?

3. What happens when witnessing turns into condemnation of non-Christians?

4. What questions can arouse curiosity about Christianity?

PARENT PAGE

- Distribute page to parents.

TEAM EFFORT—JUNIOR HIGH/MIDDLE SCHOOL (15-20 MINUTES)

THE RAGMAN

- Give each student a copy of "The Ragman" on pages 59 to 63 and a pen or pencil, or display a copy using an overhead projector.
- Read aloud the story.
- As a whole group, discuss the questions.

1. What do you think of this story?

2. What makes the story of the Ragman so powerful?

3. How does the person of Jesus relate to the Ragman story?

4. How can we put into practice the meaning of this story and share the love of God with those who aren't Christians?

TEAM EFFORT—HIGH SCHOOL (15-20 MINUTES)

MEETING PEOPLE'S NEEDS

- Divide students into groups of three or four.
- Give each student a copy of "Meeting People's Needs" on page 65 and a pen or pencil.
- Students complete page.

For each of the following types of people, determine what special needs they would have and how you could help meet the needs.

	Needs	How You Could Meet the Needs
People living in a third-world country:		
Affluent people:		
Kids living in a foster home:		
The school valedictorian:		
The most unpopular kid at school:		
Someone just like your best friend:		

How would your actions affect their openness to the gospel?

IN THE WORD (25-30 MINUTES)

SHARING THE GOOD NEWS

- Divide students into groups of three or four.
- Give each student a copy of "Sharing the Good News" on pages 67 to 73 and a pen or pencil.
- Students complete Bible study.
- Read John 4:4-26,39-42.

I. A Look at the Story

This section of Scripture is very important. These words of Jesus are significant, and the example of His life is even more exceptional. In this portion of the gospel, Jesus shares His faith and life with a Samaritan woman. It was almost unthinkable for a Jew to speak with a Samaritan and definitely unheard of for a Jewish rabbi to speak to a woman—much less a Samaritan woman. Yet we find Jesus not only speaking to her but also asking to share a drink of water and caring for her spiritual relationship with God.

A. **Why do you suppose the woman was so surprised that Jesus asked her for a drink of water? (See verses 7-9.)**
(She was a Samaritan and He was a Jew. Samaritans and Jews did not associate with each other.)

B. **What do you think Jesus means by "living water"? (See verses 10-15.)**
(Water that satisfies all thirst. Eternal life through Jesus.)

C. **What do you suppose Jesus was trying to accomplish from the conversation in verses 16-26?**
(He was trying to let the woman know He knew her and knew her needs.)

D. **What makes the declaration of Jesus in verse 26 one of the key statements of all Scripture?**
(Jesus is declaring that He is the Messiah.)

E. **List a couple of reasons why the Samaritans in the town of Sychar believed. (See verses 39-42.)**
(Because of the women's testimony and because they heard Jesus for themselves.)

II. Witnessing and You

We can observe how Jesus related to this woman and immediately see several important principles for sharing our faith with others.

A. **Meet people on their territory.**
She wasn't going to come out to see Jesus, so He came to see her. He immediately shared a common interest: water! Who of your friends or family might need you to share your faith with them? List below, their names, how you could meet them on their territory and what a common interest might be.

	Name	The Interaction	Common Interest
Example	John	Going to a baseball game	Sports

B. **Arouse curiosity about the faith.**
1. From this entire section of Scripture, how did Jesus arouse the woman's curiosity?
(He met her at a real need, water, with an answer to her unknown need, eternal life in Jesus.)
2. What are specific ways through conversation and lifestyle you can cause people to be more curious about faith in Jesus?

C. **Don't be condemning.**
Notice that Jesus did not condemn but rather cultivated the conversation by speaking truthfully to her own life. He

WARM UP

GOD AND YOU

What is one of your first memories of hearing about God?

....

....

....

What people have been positive spiritual influences in your life?

....

....

....

When did God become real in your life? (If you aren't sure if He has, it's okay to share that.)

....

....

....

TEAM EFFORT

THE RAGMAN[1]

I saw a strange sight. I stumbled upon a story most strange, like nothing my life, my street sense, my sly tongue had ever prepared me for.

Hush, child. Hush, now, and I will tell it to you.

Even before the dawn one Friday morning I noticed a young man, handsome and strong, walking on the alleys of our City. He was pulling an old cart filled with clothes both bright and new, and he was calling in a clear, tenor voice: "Rags!"

"Now, this is a wonder," I thought to myself, for the man stood six-feet-four, and his arms were like tree limbs, hard and muscular, and his eyes flashing intelligence. Could he find no better job than this, to be a ragman in the inner city?

I followed him. My curiosity drove me. And I wasn't disappointed.

Soon the Ragman saw a woman sitting on her back porch. She was sobbing into a handkerchief, sighing, and shedding a thousand tears. Her knees and elbows made a sad X. Her shoulders shook. Her heart was breaking.

The Ragman stopped his cart. Quietly, he walked to the woman, stepping round tin cans, dead toys and Pampers.

"Give me your rag," he said so gently, "and I'll give you another."

He slipped the handkerchief from her eyes. She looked up, and he laid across her palm a linen cloth so clean and new that it shined. She blinked from the gift to the giver.

Then, as he began to pull his cart again, the Ragman did a strange thing: he began to weep, to sob as grievously as she had done, his shoulders shaking. Yet she was left without a tear.

"This is a wonder," I breathed to myself, and followed the sobbing Ragman like a child who cannot turn away from mystery.

"Rags! Rags! New rags for old!"

In a little while, when the sky showed grey behind the rooftops and I could see the shredded curtains hanging out black windows, the Ragman came upon a girl whose head was wrapped in a bandage, whose eyes were empty. Blood soaked her bandage. A single line of blood ran down her cheek.

Now the tall Ragman looked upon this child with pity, and he drew a lovely yellow bonnet from his cart.

"Give me your rag," he said, tracing his own line of her cheek, "and I'll give you mine."

The child could only gaze at him while he loosened the bandage, removed it, and tied it to his own head. The bonnet he set on hers. And I gasped at what I saw for with the bandage went the wound! Against his brow it ran a darker, more substantial blood—his own!

"Rags! Rags! I take old rags!" cried the sobbing, bleeding, strong, intelligent Ragman.

The sun hurt both the sky, now, and my eyes; the Ragman seemed more and more to hurry.

"Are you going to work?" he asked a man who leaned against a telephone pole. The man shook his head.

The ragman pressed him: "Do you have a job?"

"Are you crazy?" sneered the other. He pulled away from the pole, revealing the right sleeve of his jacket—flat, the cuff stuffed into the pocket. He had no arm.

"So," said the Ragman. "Give me your jacket, and I'll give you mine."

Team Effort

Such quiet authority in his voice!

The one-armed man took off his jacket. So did the Ragman—and I trembled at what I saw: For the Ragman's arm stayed in its sleeve, and when the other put it on he had two good arms, thick as tree limbs; but the Ragman had only one.

"Go to work," he said.

After that he found a drunk, lying unconscious beneath an army blanket, an old man, hunched, wizened, and sick. He took that blanket and wrapped it around himself, but for the drunk he left new clothes.

And now I had to run to keep up with the Ragman. Though he was weeping uncontrollably, and bleeding freely at the forehead, pulling his cart with one arm, stumbling from drunkenness, falling again and again, exhausted, old, old and sick, yet he went with terrible speed. On spider's legs he skittered through the alleys of the City, this mile and the next, until he came to its limits, and then he rushed beyond.

I wept to see the change in this man. I hurt to see his sorrow. And yet I needed to see where he was going in such haste, perhaps to know what drove him so.

The little Ragman—he came to a landfill. He came to the garbage pits. And then I wanted to help him in what he did, but I hung back, hiding. He climbed a hill. With tormented labor he cleared a little space on that hill. Then he sighed. He lay down. He pillowed his head on a handkerchief and a jacket. He covered his bones with an army blanket and he died.

Oh, how I cried to witness that death! I slumped in a junked car and wailed and mourned as one who has no hope—because I had come to love the Ragman. Every other face had faded in the wonder of this man, and I cherished him; but he died. I sobbed myself to sleep.

I did not know—how could I know?—That I slept through Friday night and Saturday and its night, too.

But then, on Sunday morning, I was awakened by a violence.

Light—pure, hard, demanding light—slammed against my sour face, and I blinked, and I looked, and I saw the last and the first wonder of all. There was the Ragman, folding the blanket most carefully, a scar on his forehead, but alive! And, besides that, healthy! There was no sign of sorrow nor of age, and all the rags that he had gathered shined for cleanliness.

Well, then I lowered my head and trembling for all that I had seen, I myself walked up to the Ragman. I told him my name with shame, for I was a sorry figure next to him. Then I took off all my clothes in that place, and I said to him with a dear yearning in my voice: "Dress me."

He dressed me. My Lord, he put new rags on me, and I am a wonder beside him. The Ragman, the Ragman, the Christ!

1. What do you think of this story?

....

....

....

TEAM EFFORT

2. What makes the story of the Ragman so powerful?

....

....

....

3. How does the person of Jesus relate to the Ragman story?

....

....

....

4. How can we put into practice the meaning of this story and share the love of God with those who aren't Christians?

....

....

....

....

Note

1. Walter Wanagerin, Jr., *Ragman and Other Cries of Faith* (San Francisco, CA: Harper and Row, 1984).
   Used by permission.

TEAM EFFORT

MEETING PEOPLE'S NEEDS

For each of the following types of people, determine what special needs they would have and how you could help meet the needs.

	Needs	How You Could Meet the Needs
People living in a third world country:		
Affluent people:		
Kids living in a foster home:		
The school valedictorian:		
The most unpopular kid at school:		
Someone just like your best friend:		

How would your actions affect their openness to the gospel?

....

....

....

IN THE WORD

SHARING THE GOOD NEWS

Now he had to go through Samaria. So he came to a town in Samaria called Sychar, near the plot of ground Jacob had given to his son Joseph. Jacob's well was there, and Jesus, tired as he was from the journey, sat down by the well. It was about the sixth hour.

When a Samaritan woman came to draw water, Jesus said to her, "Will you give me a drink?" (His disciples had gone into the town to buy food.)

The Samaritan woman said to him, "You are a Jew and I am a Samaritan woman. How can you ask me for a drink?" (For Jews do not associate with Samaritans.)

Jesus answered her, "If you knew the gift of God and who it is that asks you for a drink, you would have asked him and he would have given you living water."

"Sir," the woman said, "you have nothing to draw with and the well is deep. Where can you get this living water? Are you greater than our father Jacob, who gave us the well and drank from it himself, as did also his sons and his flocks and herds?"

Jesus answered, "Everyone who drinks this water will be thirsty again, but whoever drinks the water I give him will never thirst. Indeed, the water I give him will become in him a spring of water welling up to eternal life."

The woman said to him, "Sir, give me this water so that I won't get thirsty and have to keep coming here to draw water."

He told her, "Go, call you husband and come back."

"I have no husband," she replied.

Jesus said to her, "You are right when you say you have no husband. The fact is, you have had five husbands, and the man you now have is not your husband. What you have just said is quite true."

"Sir," the woman said, "I can see that you are a prophet. Our fathers worshiped on this mountain, but you Jews claim that the place where we must worship is in Jerusalem."

Jesus declared, "Believe me, woman, a time is coming when you will worship the Father neither on this mountain nor in Jerusalem. You Samaritans worship what you do not know; we worship what we do know, for salvation is from the Jews. Yet a time is coming and has now come when the true worshipers will worship the Father in spirit and truth, for they are the kind of worshipers the Father seeks. God is spirit, and his worshipers must worship in spirit and in truth."

The woman said, "I know that Messiah" (called Christ) "is coming. When he comes, he will explain everything to us."

Then Jesus declared, "I who speak to you am he" (John 4:4-26).

Many of the Samaritans from that town believed in him because of the woman's testimony, "He told me everything I ever did." So when the Samaritans came to him, they urged him to stay with them, and he stayed two days. And because of his words many more became believers.

They said to the woman, "We no longer believe just because of what you said; now we have heard for ourselves, and we know that this man really is the Savior of the world" (John 4:39-42).

IN THE WORD

I. A Look at the Story

This section of Scripture is very important. These words of Jesus are significant and the example of His life is even more exceptional. In this portion of the gospel, Jesus shares His faith and life with a Samaritan woman. It was almost unthinkable for a Jew to speak with a Samaritan and definitely unheard of for a Jewish rabbi to speak to a woman—much less a Samaritan woman. Yet we find Jesus not only speaking to her but asking to share a drink of water and caring for her spiritual relationship with God.

A. Why do you suppose the woman was so surprised that Jesus asked her for a drink of water? (See verses 7-9.)

....

....

....

B. What do you think Jesus means by "living water"? (See verses 10-15.)

....

....

....

C. What do you suppose Jesus was trying to accomplish from the conversation in verses 16-26?

....

....

....

D. What makes the declaration of Jesus in verse 26 one of the key statements of all Scripture?

....

....

....

E. List a couple of reasons why the Samaritans in the town of Sychar believed. (See verses 39-42.)

....

....

II. Witnessing and You[1]

We can observe how Jesus related to this woman and immediately see several important principles for sharing our faith with others.

A. Meet people on their territory.

She wasn't going to come out to see Jesus, so He came to see her. He immediately shared a common interest: water! Who of your friends or family might need you to share your

faith with them? **List below, their names, how you could meet them on their territory and what a common interest might be.**

	Name	The Interaction	Common Interest
Example	John	Going to a baseball game	Sports

....

....

....

B. Arouse curiosity about the faith.

   1. From this entire section of Scripture, how did Jesus arouse the woman's curiosity?

....

....

....

   2. What are specific ways through conversation and lifestyle you can cause people to be more curious about faith in Jesus?

....

....

....

C. Don't be condemning.

   Notice that Jesus did not condemn but rather cultivated the conversation by speaking truthfully to her own life. He pointed her to her real need without condemning her. John 4:16-21 is a wonderful example of Jesus leading someone to the truth. He did it without condemning or without getting sidetracked with secondary issues. Summarize in your own words how Jesus led the conversation.

   1. Why would condemning her not have helped His relationship with her?

....

....

....

   2. In this conversation (verses 16-21), she began to get sidetracked. How did Jesus lead her back to the central issue?

....

....

....

3. What are some ways you can let people know you care for them even when you disapprove of their lifestyles?

....

....

....

D. Give people a positive encounter with the person of Jesus Christ.
   Jesus confronted the woman with the fact that He was the Messiah. Now she must respond.

   1. What are some ways you can help your friends and family have a positive encounter with the person of Jesus Christ?

   ....

   ....

   ....

   2. What are the results shown in John 4:39-42 of Jesus' conversation with the Samaritan woman?

   ....

   ....

So WHAT?

Now go back to your common interest/sharing your faith list and jot the names of two people who you will actively pursue to love, minister and share your faith with.

Name	What you plan to do	When will you begin?

Note

1. I am grateful to Fritz Ridenour and his excellent book *Tell It Like It Is* (Ventura, CA: Regal Books, 1968) for first introducing me to these principles in a different form.

THINGS TO THINK ABOUT

1. Why are some Christians afraid to share their faith?

....

....

....

2. What attracted you to Christianity?

....

....

....

3. What happens when witnessing turns into condemnation of non-Christians?

....

....

....

4. What questions can arouse curiosity about Christianity?

....

....

....

PARENT PAGE

EARNING THE RIGHT TO BE HEARD

Have you ever heard the phrase, "Jesus is the answer"? Most likely you have. As Christians, we know that statement to be true. Yet the unbeliever has not even asked the question. Sometimes we are giving the answer to an unasked question. Lloyd Ogilvie has said, "We ought to be living such a radiant life that it prompts the question, 'Why are you the way you are?' and opens the way for a positive answer of what God has done. There's nothing more silly than the answer to an unasked question. That's witnessing of the lowest order. But there's nothing more powerful and contagious than the answer to a sincere question about the source of our quality of life. That's witnessing of the highest order."

Our life and actions are our greatest witness. We must earn the right to be heard, and then speak the truths of Jesus Christ.

What did Jesus tell Peter and Andrew in Matthew 4:18-20?

....

....

The fishing illustration is perfect for witnessing. When you fish you must put bait on the hook, and wait. As a Christian, your life is the bait that will arouse curiosity. Seldom do you catch fish by harpooning them or waiting for the fish to jump out of the water onto your lap. Get the message?
Here are four thought-provoking questions for you to answer.

1. What would the world be like if every Christian was like you in personality and attitude?

....

....

2. Would you like to reproduce what has happened to your faith in the lives of others?

....

....

3. Would you like everyone to discover what you have found?

....

....

4. If you were arrested for being a Christian, would there be enough evidence to convict you?

....

....

....

Session 3 "A Lifestyle of Love Helps"
Date ....

Read Paul's thrilling testimony before King Agrippa and the governor in Acts 26.

What points stand out in your mind about Paul's testimony?

....

....

....

Reread Acts 26:24-29. This is where the conversation gets pretty intense. What are your feelings about Paul's statement to the king in verses 28, 29?

☐   Right on, Paul!
☐   Sounds boastful to me.
☐   I would be afraid to say such things.
☐   Let me at them.
☐   I'm not sure I understand.

Answer these two questions:

1. What can we as a family do to be a better witness to our nonbelieving family members and friends?

....

....

....

2. Who can we love through action in our family or friends, and what can we do to begin ministering to them?

....

....

....

....

Session 3 "A Lifestyle of Love Helps"
Date ....

DISCIPLESHIP

KEY VERSE

"Then he called the crowd to him along with his disciples and said: 'If anyone would come after me, he must deny himself and take up his cross and follow me.'"
Mark 8:34

BIBLICAL BASIS

Mark 8:34-37;
Galatians 2:20

THE BIG IDEA

Discipleship is obediently denying yourself and following the Lord Jesus Christ.

AIMS OF THIS SESSION

During this session you will guide students to:

• Examine the key principles of being a disciple of Jesus Christ;

• Discover what it means to follow after Jesus Christ;

• Implement a decision to submit their lives to the lordship of Jesus Christ.

WARM UP

What Would You Do?—
Students decide what they would do under pressure.

TEAM EFFORT— JUNIOR HIGH/ MIDDLE SCHOOL

The Cost of Living—
Students brainstorm the cost of different activities.

TEAM EFFORT— HIGH SCHOOL

A Committed Disciple—
A look at the commitment of a communist student.

IN THE WORD

Totally Committed—
A Bible study on what it means to follow Jesus.

THINGS TO THINK ABOUT (OPTIONAL)

Questions to get students thinking and talking about the cost of discipleship.

PARENT PAGE

A tool to get the session into the home and allow parents and young people to discuss being committed to Jesus.

LEADER'S DEVOTIONAL

"We asked people if they would do any of the following for 10 million dollars. Two-thirds would agree to at least one, some to several: Abandon their entire family (25%). Abandon their church (25%). Become prostitutes for a week or more (23%). Leave their spouses (16%). Kill a stranger (7%). Change their race (6%). Put their children up for adoption (3%)."—survey from *The Day America Told the Truth*

What would you be willing to do for 10 million dollars? Imagine all the wonderful things you could do with 10 million dollars. Vacations! A new Porsche! Throw in a Ferrari or two! What about that mansion you've had your eye on? Ten million dollars could go a long way! But even if you had that much money, there'd still be a cost. A major cost and that's the challenge of this lesson: Are you willing to sell out or be sold out for Jesus Christ?

The goal of discipleship is to daily walk with Jesus. To do that, Jesus asks you to do two things: 1) Deny yourself 2) Take up your cross. If you are going to continue to follow Jesus, what area of your life do you need to hand over to God? What problem, sin or temptations do you need to lay at the foot of the Cross today? Following Jesus is costly because it means following God's will and not our own.

Besides denying ourselves, taking up our cross isn't a very popular idea either. The cross is an instrument of death. A rugged piece of wood that criminals guilty of their crimes against the state were nailed to. In taking up your cross to follow Jesus, what needs to die so that you can experience new life in Christ? What struggles or hardships must you bear in the name of Christ?

The good news of the gospel is that because of Christ's death on the cross and resurrection from the dead, you don't have to bear your cross alone. Jesus is the one who gives you strength to deny yourself in order to know His love more fully. He is the one who will help you bear your cross as you follow Him. Don't let anyone tell you that following Jesus isn't costly, but don't let anyone tell you it's not worth it. Ten million dollars can only go so far. And at what cost? (Written by Joey O'Connor.)

SESSION FOUR

BIBLE *TUCK - IN*™

DISCIPLESHIP

KEY VERSE

"Then he called the crowd to him along with his disciples and said: 'If anyone would come after me, he must deny himself and take up his cross and follow me.'" Mark 8:34

BIBLICAL BASIS

Mark 8:34-37; Galatians 2:20

THE BIG IDEA

Discipleship is obediently denying yourself and following the Lord Jesus Christ.

WARM UP (5-10 Minutes)

WHAT WOULD YOU DO?

- Divide students into pairs.
- Display a copy of "What Would You Do?" on page 85 using an overhead projector.
- Students complete the page.

Hitler banished all professing Christians from his government because he said their loyalty to the state was endangered by their loyalty to Christianity. If you were a government employee in Germany during the 1940s would you:

- ☐ Be first to go?
- ☐ Think about leaving?
- ☐ Leave eventually?
- ☐ Quit if it got bad?
- ☐ Have a secure job?
- Why?

TEAM EFFORT—JUNIOR HIGH/ MIDDLE SCHOOL (15-20 Minutes)

THE COST OF LIVING

- Divide students into groups of three or four.
- Give each student a copy of "The Cost of Living" on page 87 and a pen or pencil.
- Students complete page.

Then he called the crowd to him along with his disciples and said: "If anyone would come after me, he must deny himself and take up his cross and follow me. For whoever wants to save his life will lose it, but whoever loses his life for me and for the gospel will save it. What good is it for a man to gain the whole world, yet forfeit his soul? Or what can a man give in exchange for his soul?" (Mark 8:34–37).

What does it take to come after Jesus?

1. **Deny yourself.**
   You belong to Christ, not yourself. You were bought for a high price. In order to follow Christ there is a sense of denial of your own needs for the sake of Christ's purposes.
   a. What does Paul say in Galatians 2:20 about denying yourself?
      (Your life is no longer yours but Christ's.)
   b. How does Galatians 2:20 apply to your life?

2. **Take up your cross.**
   a. What does it mean to "take up your cross"?
      (To bear what's required of you to follow Christ.)
   b. Are you willing to accept the cost of becoming Christ's person in your home, school, love life and relationships with your parents?
   c. You've listed ways as a group, but now list specific ways you can take up your cross in the above situations.

3. **Follow me.**
   a. Following Jesus means to be willing to go anywhere and do anything for Him. Are you willing to follow Jesus wherever He leads you?
      ☐ Yes   ☐ No   ☐ Not Sure
   b. What item, attitude or priority could you list under each heading to show obedience to that part of the Scripture?

Deny Yourself	Take Up Your Cross	Follow Me

SO WHAT?

Are you passionately pursuing Christ? On a scale from 1 to 10, mark an *X* where you see yourself today.

1   2   3   4   5   6   7   8   9   10

Not at All   Total Commitment

What will it take for you to give more of your time and attention to passionately pursuing Christ? (This is the most important question of this session.)

THINGS TO THINK ABOUT (OPTIONAL)

- Use the questions on page 95 after or as a part of "In the Word."
1. What makes discipleship costly?

2. Why is it so difficult to deny ourselves, take up our cross and follow Jesus?

3. Give illustrations of people who have gained all the world has to offer but don't have the blessings of a relationship with God.

PARENT PAGE

- Distribute page to parents.

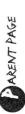

Brainstorm activities or events that fit the following categories:

Five activities for free

1. ...
2. ...
3. ...
4. ...
5. ...

Three activities for $1 - $20

1. ...
2. ...
3. ...

Three activities for $20 - $100

1. ...
2. ...
3. ...

Three activities for over $100

1. ...
2. ...
3. ...

Now fill out the list below:

Five aspects of the Christian life that are free

1. ...
2. ...
3. ...

Three aspects of the Christian life that are costly, but not too costly

1. ...
2. ...
3. ...
4. ...
5. ...

Three costly aspects of the Christian life

1. ...
2. ...
3. ...

Three extremely costly aspects of the Christian life

1. ...
2. ...
3. ...

"Some events in life are free while others are costly." How does that phrase relate to our Christian lives?

Fold

TEAM EFFORT—HIGH SCHOOL (15-20 MINUTES)

A COMMITTED DISCIPLE

- Display a copy of "A Committed Disciple" on page 89 using an overhead projector.
- Read aloud the letter.
- Students answer questions.
- As a whole group, discuss students' responses.

The following is a letter from a communist student who is breaking his engagement with his fiancee. While reading this letter, think of how his commitment and dedication to communism compares to our commitment and dedication to Jesus Christ.

The communist student wrote:

"We communists have a high casualty rate. We are the ones who get shot and hung and ridiculed and fired from our jobs and in every other way made as uncomfortable as possible. A certain percentage of us get killed or imprisoned. We live in virtual poverty. We turn back to the party every penny we make above what is absolutely necessary to keep us alive. We communists do not have the time or the money for many movies, or concerts, or T-bone steaks, or decent homes, or new cars. We have been described as fanatics. We are fanatics. Our lives are dominated by one great overshadowing factor: The struggle for world communism. We communists have a philosophy of life that no amount of money can buy. We have a cause to fight for, a definite purpose in life. We subordinate our petty personal selves into great movement of humanity; and if our personal lives seem hard or our egos appear to suffer through subordination to the party, then we are adequately compensated by the thought that each of us in his small way is contributing to something new and true and better for mankind.

"There is one thing in which I am in dead earnest about, and that is the communist cause. It is my life, my business, my religion, my hobby, my sweetheart, my wife, and my mistress, my breath and meat. I work at it in the daytime and dream of it at night. Its hold on me grows, not lessens, as time goes on; therefore, I cannot carry on a friendship, a love affair, or even a conversation without relating it to this force that both drives and guides my life. I evaluate people, books, ideas and actions according to how they affect the communist cause, and by their attitude toward it. I've already ben in jail because of my ideals, and if necessary, I'm ready to go before a firing squad."

What are your thoughts about this letter?

Does the student's commitment relate in any way to our Christian lives? How?

Can you think of any Scriptures that might relate to this letter?

IN THE WORD (25-30 MINUTES)

TOTALLY COMMITTED

- Divide students into groups of three or four.
- Give each student a copy of "Totally Committed" on pages 91 and 93 and a pen or pencil, or display a copy using an overhead projector.
- Students complete the Bible study.

WARM UP

WHAT WOULD YOU DO?

Hitler banished all professing Christians from his government because he said their loyalty to the state was endangered by their loyalty to Christianity. If you were a government employee in Germany during the 1940s would you:

☐ Be first to go?

☐ Think about leaving?

☐ Leave eventually?

☐ Quit if it got bad?

☐ Have a secure job?

Why?

....

....

....

TEAM EFFORT

THE COST OF LIVING

Brainstorm activities or events that fit the following categories:

Five activities for free

1.
2.
3.
4.
5.

Three activities for $1 - $20

1.
2.
3.

Three activities for $20 - $100

1.
2.
3.

Three activities for over $100

1.
2.
3.

Now fill out the list below:
Five aspects of the Christian life that are free

1.
2.
3.
4.
5.

Three aspects of the Christian life that are costly, but not too costly

1.
2.
3.

Three costly aspects of the Christian life

1.
2.
3.

Three extremely costly aspects of the Christian life

1.
2.
3.

"Some events in life are free while others are costly." How does that phrase relate to our Christian lives?

TEAM EFFORT

A COMMITTED DISCIPLE

The following is a letter from a communist student who is breaking his engagement with his fiancee. While reading this letter, think of how his commitment and dedication to communism compares to our commitment and dedication to Jesus Christ.

The communist student wrote:

"We communists have a high casualty rate. We are the ones who get shot and hung and ridiculed and fired from our jobs and in every other way made as uncomfortable as possible. A certain percentage of us get killed or imprisoned. We live in virtual poverty. We turn back to the party every penny we make above what is absolutely necessary to keep us alive. We communists do not have the time or the money for many movies, or concerts, or T-bone steaks, or decent homes, or new cars. We have been described as fanatics. We are fanatics. Our lives are dominated by one great overshadowing factor: The struggle for world communism. We communists have a philosophy of life that no amount of money can buy. We have a cause to fight for, a definite purpose in life. We subordinate our petty personal selves into great movement of humanity; and if our personal lives seem hard or our egos appear to suffer through subordination to the party, then we are adequately compensated by the thought that each of us in his small way is contributing to something new and true and better for mankind.

"There is one thing in which I am in dead earnest about, and that is the communist cause. It is my life, my business, my religion, my hobby, my sweetheart, my wife, and my mistress, my breath and meat. I work at it in the daytime and dream of it at night. Its hold on me grows, not lessens, as time goes on; therefore, I cannot carry on a friendship, a love affair, or even a conversation without relating it to this force that both drives and guides my life. I evaluate people, books, ideas and actions according to how they affect the communist cause, and by their attitude toward it. I've already been in jail because of my ideals, and if necessary, I'm ready to go before a firing squad."

What are your thoughts about this letter?

....

....

....

Does the student's commitment relate in any way to our Christian lives? How?

....

....

....

Can you think of any Scriptures that might relate to this letter?

....

....

IN THE WORD

TOTALLY COMMITTED

Then he called the crowd to him along with his disciples and said: "If anyone would come after me, he must deny himself and take up his cross and follow me. For whoever wants to save his life will lose it, but whoever loses his life for me and for the gospel will save it. What good is it for a man to gain the whole world, yet forfeit his soul? Or what can a man give in exchange for his soul?" (Mark 8:34-37).

What does it take to come after Jesus?

....

....

1. Deny yourself.

You belong to Christ, not yourself. You were bought for a high price. In order to follow Christ there is a sense of denial of your own needs for the sake of Christ's purposes.

a. What does Paul say in Galatians 2:20 about denying yourself?

....

....

....

b. How does Galatians 2:20 apply to your life?

....

....

....

2. Take up your cross.

a. What does it mean to "take up your cross"?

....

....

....

b. Are you willing to accept the cost of becoming Christ's person in your home, school, love life and relationships with your parents?

....

....

....

IN THE WORD

c. You've listed ways as a group, but now list specific ways you can take up your cross in the above situations.

....
....
....

3. Follow me.

a. Following Jesus means to be willing to go anywhere and do anything for Him. Are you willing to follow Jesus wherever He leads you?

☐ Yes   ☐ No   ☐ Not Sure

b. What item, attitude or priority could you list under each heading to show obedience to that part of the Scripture?

<u>Deny Yourself</u>   <u>Take Up Your Cross</u>   <u>Follow Me</u>

....
....
....

SO WHAT?

Are you passionately pursuing Christ? On a scale from 1 to 10, mark an *X* where you see yourself today.

| 1 | 2 | 3 | 4 | 5 | 6 | 7 | 8 | 9 | 10 |

Not at All   Total Commitment

What will it take for you to give more of your time and attention to passionately pursuing Christ? (This is the most important question of this session.)

....
....
....
....

Things to Think About

1. What makes discipleship costly?

....

....

....

2. Why is it so difficult to deny ourselves, take up our cross and follow Jesus?

....

....

....

3. Give illustrations of people who have gained all the world has to offer but don't have the blessings of a relationship with God.

....

....

....

PARENT PAGE

LINDA

Here's a case study that may open good discussion on the cost of discipleship.

Linda was a leader in the youth group. Her faith and her enthusiasm for God and the group had been an inspiration for several years. During her senior year in high school she started to waiver in her lifestyle. Many in the youth group had heard rumors that Linda was experimenting with drugs and alcohol. When it came to sexual purity, her new boyfriend was known around the school as someone who wouldn't take no for an answer. Some of the concerned students in the youth group got together with one of the youth workers to discuss whether Linda should still be in the youth group leadership core.

Together discuss how you would handle Linda.

If Linda decided to make a deepened commitment to Christ, what advice would you give her to become a disciple of Christ?

....

....

There is a cost to being a disciple of Jesus Christ, but the rewards are well worth it. A very successful business executive once said, "I spent my entire life climbing the corporate ladder only to find that when I got to the top, my ladder was leaning against the wrong building. I have wasted my life with trivia."

How do the words of this business executive seem similar to the words of Jesus in Mark 8:35-37?

....

....

....

Session 4 "Discipleship" Date ....

SETTING A STRONG FOUNDATION

LEADER'S PEP TALK

A little over six years ago our little daughter Heidi Michelle was born with a major heart complication. It was really, really hard. Yet, in the midst of our pain, worry and exhaustion, Cathy and I were overwhelmed with the love and support of our church and the youth ministry community. To say it was eventful is an understatement. People gave us an incredible amount of love and support. However, the best piece of advice came to me over lunch with a friend of mine a few months after Heidi's birth. He works as a real estate developer, but actually he's a philosopher. Toby shook my hand, looked me square in the face and said, "Burnsie, nobody said it would be easy."

His greeting has stayed with me for the last six years. He's right you know. God never promised to remove the burdens or take away the pain of living. He did promise to walk with us through the problems.

The theme of this section is the incredible words of Jesus at the end of His Sermon on the Mount:

> Therefore everyone who hears these words of mine and
> puts them into practice is like a wise man who built his
> house on the rock. The rain came down, the streams rose,
> and the winds blew and beat against that house; yet it did
> not fall, because it had its foundation on the rock. But
> everyone who hear these words of mine and does not put
> them into practice is like a foolish man who built his house
> on sand. The rain came down, the streams rose, and the
> winds blew and beat against that house, and it fell with a
> great crash (Matthew 7:24-27).

The eternal truth of these words of Jesus is that rain, wind and storms will come to everyone's life, and the person who builds their life on the Rock will make it and the ones who don't will crash.

I like what Gail McDonald once said, "Untended fires soon become nothing but a pile of ashes." This section is about tending the spiritual fires of your students. Part of any good youth program is not *just* telling them about Jesus but helping these young Christians build up a solid enough faith to stand when the storms of life come—and the storms will come.

You may be like me and can't build even the simplest of houses. But we are about building spiritual truths into the lives of students, and that's the most important factor of all. I doubt if your kids will remember the setting of your group and I know they won't remember this curriculum. Yet, we have the awesome opportunity and privilege to plant the Word of God in their lives. When others are trying to tear down our students, you're helping to set their foundations.

As you go about that task, remember this great promise from God:

> All men are like grass, and all their glory is like
> the flowers of the field; the grass withers and the
> flowers fall, but the word of the Lord stands for-
> ever (1 Peter 1:24,25).

SETTING A STRONG FOUNDATION

KEY VERSE

"Therefore everyone who hears these words of mine and puts them into practice is like a wise man who built his house on the rock." Matthew 7:24

BIBLICAL BASIS

Joshua 1:8;
Psalm 1:2,3; 119:105;
Matthew 6:21,24; 7:24-27;
Mark 1:35;
John 14:15,21;
Philippians 3:12-14;
1 Peter 2:4-8;
Revelation 3:20

THE BIG IDEA

When you set a solid faith foundation you will be able to withstand the trials of life.

AIMS OF THIS SESSION

During this session you will guide students to:
• Examine the importance of setting a firm faith foundation;
• Discover how to develop a lifelong faith that will be able to stand up against the world;
• Implement a commitment to develop a deeper relationship with God.

WARM UP

Your Dream Home—
Students share ideas about their dream homes.

TEAM EFFORT— JUNIOR HIGH/ MIDDLE SCHOOL

A Human Pyramid—
Students illustrate the necessity of a strong foundation.

TEAM EFFORT— HIGH SCHOOL

Set on the Rock—
An illustration of the results of a weak foundation and a strong foundation.

IN THE WORD

Principles for Setting a Strong Foundation—
A Bible study on having your life set on Jesus.

THINGS TO THINK ABOUT (OPTIONAL)

Questions to get students thinking and talking about a spiritual foundation.

PARENT PAGE

A tool to get the session into the home and allow parents and young people to discuss the results of a poor foundation.

LEADER'S DEVOTIONAL

"There is so much frustration in the world because we have relied on gods rather than God. We have genuflected before the god of science only to find that it has given us the atomic bomb, producing fears and anxieties that science can never mitigate. We have bowed before the god of money only to learn that there are such things as love and friendship that money cannot buy....These transitory gods are not able to save or bring happiness to the human heart. Only God is able. It is faith in Him that we must rediscover."—Martin Luther King, Jr.

Setting a strong foundation begins with asking Christ to be the cornerstone of our lives. It also means asking Him to remove all the "gods" in our lives. Martin Luther King, Jr.'s words remind us that, at times, even Christians have bowed, genuflected and worshiped things other than the one true God. Christ wants to be the cornerstone of our lives, but He leaves the decision up to us. How does God want to strengthen the foundation of your life?

Setting a foundation is often a long, slow process filled with delays and setbacks. It can take longer and costs more than we first anticipate. The same is true for our spiritual lives. At times, it can seem like we're stagnant and lifeless. We see no fruit of God in our lives. We grow tired, bored and frustrated of the process that God started in our lives long ago. Have you ever wondered when God is going to finish the work He started in your life? Read Philippians 1:6. God is faithful.

As you make Christ the cornerstone of your life, God promises to create a strong foundation. He promises to finish what He started. Yes, the process takes a long time, but God wants this process to last your lifetime so you can experience all He is. When you put the words of Jesus into practice, there's no storm, no problem, no obstacle you can't overcome in Christ. Jesus didn't come to take away our problems, but to give us hope and strength in our storms. The "gods" of our generation cannot save us from storms or bring us the happiness we desire. Only God is able. By rediscovering God, we will brush away the sand that covers our firm foundation in Christ. (Written by Joey O'Connor.)

SESSION FIVE

BIBLE TUCK-IN™

SETTING A STRONG FOUNDATION

KEY VERSE

"Therefore everyone who hears these words of mine and puts them into practice is like a wise man who built his house on the rock." Matthew 7:24

BIBLICAL BASIS

Joshua 1:8; Psalm 1:2,3; 119:105; Matthew 6:21,24; 7:24-27; Mark 1:35; John 14:15,21; Philippians 3:12-14; 1 Peter 2:4-8; Revelation 3:20

THE BIG IDEA

When you set a solid faith foundation you will be able to withstand the trials of life.

WARM UP (5-10 MINUTES)

YOUR DREAM HOME

• As a whole group, answer the following questions. Go around the group having each student answer the first question. Repeat with the second and third questions.

What is your favorite room in the house?

If you could build your dream home, what would it look like?

Where would your dream home be?

If you could change one thing about your home, what would it be?

---- Fold ----

---

4. Build on your foundation daily. Read Joshua 1:8 and Psalm 1:2,3.
   a. What is the result of spending time with God each day?
      (We will be prosperous when we follow God's commands.)
   b. What example does Jesus give us in Mark 1:35?
      (Jesus went off by Himself to pray.)

SO WHAT?

Here are three points to consider:

1. Is your foundation based on Jesus?

2. What do you need to do to set your foundation on Jesus?

3. Write a prayer or draw a picture expressing your need to set your foundation on Jesus or expressing your thanks to Jesus for being your foundation.

THINGS TO THINK ABOUT (OPTIONAL)

• Use the questions on page 111 after or as a part of "In the Word."

1. What one thing could you do this week to strengthen the foundation of your spiritual life?

2. Describe a time in your life when you started to set your spiritual foundation. What caused you to get serious with God?

3. What are five foundation crumblers in your life that you will have to watch out for?

4. Who in your youth group or family helps you strengthen your foundation?

PARENT PAGE

• Distribute page to parents.

A HUMAN PYRAMID

- Have students form a human pyramid. Try many different arrangements of the students.
- Then ask students:

What is necessary to build a solid pyramid?

When did we fail? When did we succeed?

How is this like building our Christian lives?

What is necessary to build a solid Christian life?

TEAM EFFORT—HIGH SCHOOL (15-20 MINUTES)

SET ON THE ROCK

- Have available a large clear plastic sack with sand in it and a large solid rock. Ask students the following questions:

What could you use sand for and what could you use rock for?

Sand is temporary and rock is permanent. Which is best for setting a foundation for a home?

Consider the list you've developed. What are the advantages and disadvantages of using sand? Of using rock?

Sand	Rock
easy to move	hard
wind and rain blow it away	solid
ever changing and shifting	permanent, lasting

How is this like our Christian lives?

How does a solid foundation help us in our spiritual growth?

IN THE WORD (25-30 MINUTES)

PRINCIPLES FOR SETTING A STRONG FOUNDATION

- Divide students into groups of three or four.
- Give each student a copy of "Principles for Setting a Strong Foundation" on pages 105 to 107 and a pen or pencil, or display a copy using an overhead projector.
- Students complete the Bible study.

Therefore everyone who hears these words of mine and puts them into practice is like a wise man who built his house on the rock. The rain came down, and the streams rose, and the winds blew and beat against that house; yet it did not fall, because it had its foundation on the rock. But everyone who hears these words of mine and does not put them into practice is like a foolish man who built his house on sand. The rain came down, the streams rose, and the winds blew and beat against that house, and it fell with a great crash (Matthew 7:24-27).

Notice that the same thing happened to each house. The rain came, the streams rose and the wind blew and beat against the house. Problems come to everyone regardless of spiritual maturity or lifestyle. The major difference is that when problems come, the person with a strong base will be able to withstand the attack. Christians are not free from problems. We must prepare for difficulties by developing a solid foundation. What's great is that you don't need to develop it on your own—God will help.

1. You need a cornerstone. A cornerstone is a stone set at the bottom of a structure. Read 1 Peter 2:4-8.
a. Who is clearly the Cornerstone in this Scripture?
(Jesus is the Cornerstone.)
b. Is this Cornerstone a part of your life?

Without the Cornerstone you can never have a strong foundation.

2. You must follow the instructions to set a strong foundation properly. Read John 14:15,21.
a. What do these verses tell us to do if we love God?
(We are to obey God's commands.)
b. What is the result of obedience in verse 21?
(Jesus will love those who obey Him and reveal Himself to them.)
c. How do Jesus' statements in these verses relate to Joshua 1:8 and Psalm 1:2,3?
(These passages show that obedience to God's commands brings blessings.)

3. Set your foundation slowly. Growth is slow; growth takes time. Setting a strong foundation is a lifelong process. Slow, consistent growth is a sure way to spiritual maturity. Read Philippians 3:12-14.
How do you think these wise words of Paul deal with setting a strong foundation slowly?
(Growth is a process that we need to consistently work on.)

IN THE WORD

PRINCIPLES FOR SETTING A STRONG FOUNDATION

> Therefore everyone who hears these words of mine and puts them into practice is like a wise man who built his house on the rock. The rain came down, and the streams rose, and the winds blew and beat against that house; yet it did not fall, because it had its foundation on the rock. But everyone who hears these words of mine and does not put them into practice is like a foolish man who built his house on sand. The rain came down, the streams rose, and the winds blew and beat against that house, and it fell with a great crash (Matthew 7:24-27).

Notice that the same thing happened to each house. The rain came, the streams rose and the wind blew and beat against the house. Problems come to everyone regardless of spiritual maturity or lifestyle. The major difference is that when problems come, the person with a strong base will be able to withstand the attack.

Christians are not free from problems. We must prepare for difficulties by developing a solid foundation. What's great is that you don't need to develop it on your own—God will help.

1. **You need a cornerstone. A cornerstone is a stone set at the bottom of a structure. Read 1 Peter 2:4-8.**
   a. **Who is clearly the Cornerstone in this Scripture?**

   ....
   ....
   ....

   b. **Is this Cornerstone a part of your life?**

   ....
   ....
   ....

   Without the Cornerstone you can never have a strong foundation.

 IN THE WORD

2. You must follow the instructions to set a strong foundation properly. Read John 14:15,21.

   a. What do these verses tell us to do if we love God?

   ....

   ....

   ....

   b. What is the result of obedience in verse 21?

   ....

   ....

   ... .

   c. How do Jesus' statements in these verses relate to Joshua 1:8 and Psalm 1:2,3?

   ....

   ....

   ....

3. Set your foundation slowly. Growth is slow; growth takes time. Setting a strong foundation is a lifelong process. Slow, consistent growth is a sure way to spiritual maturity. Read Philippians 3:12-14.
   How do you think these wise words of Paul deal with setting a strong foundation slowly?

   ....

   ....

   ....

4. Build on your foundation daily. Read Joshua 1:8 and Psalm 1:2,3.
   a. What is the result of spending time with God each day?

   ....

   ....

   ....

   b. What example does Jesus give us in Mark 1:35?

   ....

   ....

   ....

So WHAT?

Here are three points to consider:

1. Is your foundation based on Jesus?

....

....

....

2. What do you need to do to set your foundation on Jesus?

....

....

....

3. Write a prayer or draw a picture expressing your need to set your foundation on Jesus or expressing your thanks to Jesus
   for being your foundation.

....

....

....

THINGS TO THINK ABOUT

1. What one thing could you do this week to strengthen the foundation of your spiritual life?

....

....

....

2. Describe a time in your life when you started to set your spiritual foundation. What caused you to get serious with God?

....

....

....

3. What are five foundation crumblers in your life that you will have to watch out for?

....

....

....

4. Who in your youth group or family helps you strengthen your foundation?

....

....

....

PARENT PAGE

In 1923 a very important meeting was held at the Edgewater Beach Hotel in Chicago. Attending this meeting were nine of the world's most successful financiers: Charles Schwab, steel magnate; Samuel Insull, president of the largest utility company; Howard Hopson, president of the largest gas company; Arthur Cotton, the greatest wheat speculator; Richard Whitney, president of the New York Stock Exchange; Albert Fall, a member of the president's cabinet; Leon Fraser, president of the Bank of International Settlements; Jesse Livermore, the great "bear" on Wall Street; and Ivar Krueger, head of the most powerful monopoly.

Twenty-five years later, Charles Schwab had died in bankruptcy, having lived on borrowed money for five years before his death; Samuel Insull had died a fugitive from justice and penniless in a foreign land; Howard Hopson was insane; Arthur Cotton had died abroad, insolvent; Richard Whitney had spent time in Sing Sing Prison; Albert Fall had been pardoned so that he could die at home; Jesse Livermore, Ivar Krueger and Leon Fraser had all died by suicide. All of these men had learned well the art of making a living, but none of them had learned HOW TO LIVE![1]

1. What was the basis of these men's lives?

....

....

....

2. What was missing in all of these men's lives? Why is it so easy to slide into the same kinds of goals as these men?

....

....

....

3. What does Matthew 6:21,24 mean for you today?

....

....

....

4. How do these Scriptures relate to setting a firm spiritual foundation?

....

....

....

Note

1. Jim Burns, *Spirit Wings* (Ann Arbor, MI: Servant Publications, 1992), pp. 170-171. Used by permission.

Session 5 "Setting a Strong Foundation" Date ....

OBEDIENCE

EY VERSE

"**W**hoever has my commands and obeys them, he is the one who loves me. He who loves me will be loved by my Father, and I too will love him and show myself to him." John 14:21

BIBLICAL BASIS

1 Samuel 15:22;
John 14:21;
Philippians 2:5-11;
2 John 6

THE BIG IDEA

If there is a secret to the Christian life it is found in obedience.

AIMS OF THIS SESSION

During this session you will guide students to:

- Examine the biblical truths of obedience;
- Discover how obedience brings freedom and fulfillment;
- Implement specific action steps toward a more obedient lifestyle.

WARM UP

A Trip to Mars—
Students share what their most prized possessions are.

TEAM EFFORT— JUNIOR HIGH/ MIDDLE SCHOOL

Blondin—
A story showing what it means to act on your beliefs.

TEAM EFFORT— HIGH SCHOOL

What Would You Do?—
Students share to what degree they would be obedient.

IN THE WORD

Obedience—
A Bible study on the results of obedience.

THINGS TO THINK ABOUT (OPTIONAL)

Questions to get students thinking and talking about what it means to be obedient to God.

PARENT PAGE

A tool to get the session into the home and allow parents and young people to discuss God's call to obedience.

LEADER'S DEVOTIONAL

"If for one whole day, quietly and determinedly, we were to give ourselves up to the ownership of Jesus and to obeying His orders, we should be amazed at its close to realize all He had packed into that one day."—Oswald Chambers

Read the headlines. Catch the latest news. Flip on Oprah, Sally, Phil or Geraldo. Hear about the hottest scandal, equal rights, the environment, health care, abortion, immigration, homelessness, racism, financial misconduct, politics, war and disease. Television, radio, newspapers and magazines bombard us daily with every issue under the sun. We are "issued out" with every single cause and controversy imaginable. In the midst of this barrage of issues, stands Jesus Christ who asks of us only one thing: "Will you obey me today?"

Obedience. Only today. That's all Jesus Christ asks of us. All the noise of the day's issues distracts us from the call of Christ to listen and obey Him. John 10:27 "My sheep listen to my voice; I know them, and they follow me." Following Jesus means listening to the Shepherd's voice; the voice of Jesus who knows you and wants you to follow Him. Listening to Jesus' voice is the first step to following Him and enjoying a rich, abundant life with God.

What is distracting you from hearing the voice of God today? What has lured your attention away from obeying Christ? How can you today focus your attention only on Christ in order to hear His voice and follow Him? What areas of your life make you too hurried and rushed to hear Jesus' voice? How will listening to Jesus bring you the peace you desire?

Obedience to Christ means freedom and obedience. Begin with hearing the voice of God. God's Word is not burdensome; His commands are never too difficult to carry out. God wants to show you what remarkable things can happen when you are totally yielded to God's commands. It is for your freedom that Christ died, and it is in dying for Christ that you are truly free. (Written by Joey O'Connor.)

S E S S I O N   S I X

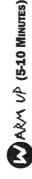

B I B L E   T U C K - I N ™

OBEDIENCE

KEY VERSE

"Whoever has my commands and obeys them, he is the one who loves me. He who loves me will be loved by my Father, and I too will love him and show myself to him." John 14:21

BIBLICAL BASIS

1 Samuel 15:22; John 14:21; Philippians 2:5-11; 2 John 6

THE BIG IDEA

If there is a secret to the Christian life it is found in obedience.

WARM UP (5-10 MINUTES)

A TRIP TO MARS

• Divide students into groups of three or four.

• Give each student a copy of "A Trip to Mars" on page 119 and a pen or pencil.

• Students complete the page.

Imagine for a moment that you have been offered an all-expense paid trip on the first spaceship to the planet Mars. It's just been discovered that there is life on this planet, and people your age. List five personal items you would take on your trip.

1. ....

2. ....

3. ....

4. ....

5. ....

Now share why you would choose these items.

....

....

- Fold -

117

---

3. Listed below are several words. With the previous Scriptures in mind, read the word and then discuss how obedience to God fits in with each area of our lives.

Servanthood	Boyfriend/Girlfriend
Parents	Parties
Sexuality	Worship
Grades	War

SO WHAT?

1. Take a few moments to list areas of your life in which God is calling you to obedience.

....

2. How will you show obedience to God in these areas?

....

....

THINGS TO THINK ABOUT (OPTIONAL)

• Use the questions on page 129 after or as a part of "In the Word."

1. How do you think the standards of our society influence our obedience to God?

....

2. God loves you! He wants the best for you! How do you think He feels when you walk away from Him in disobedience? How would you feel if you had children who were disobedient to you as a parent?

....

3. John Calvin wrote, "True knowledge of God is born out of obedience." What do you think about this statement.

....

....

PARENT PAGE

• Distribute page to parents.

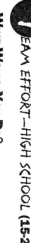

TEAM EFFORT—JUNIOR HIGH/ MIDDLE SCHOOL (15-20 MINUTES)

BLONDIN

- Give each student a copy of "Blondin" on page 121 and a pen or pencil, or display a copy using an overhead projector.
- Read aloud the story.
- Students complete the page.

Before ten thousand screaming people (he) inched his way from the Canadian side of the falls to the United States side. When he got there the crowd began shouting his name: "Blondin! Blondin! Blondin! Blondin!" Finally he raised his arms, quieted the crowd, and (how's this for an ego trip?) shouted to them, "I am Blondin! Do you believe in me?" the crowd shouted back, "We believe! We believe! We believe!"

Again he quieted the crowd, and once more he shouted to them, "I'm going back across the tightrope, but this time I'm going to carry someone on my back. Do you believe I can do that?" The crowd went dead. Nothing.

Finally out of the crowd stepped one man. He climbed on Blondin's shoulders, and for the next three-and-a-half-hours, Blondin inched his way back across the tightrope to the Canadian side of the falls.

The point of the story is blatantly clear: Ten thousand people stood there that day chanting, "We believe, we believe!" but only one person really believed! Believing is not just saying, "I accept the fact." Believing is giving your life over into the hands of the one in whom you say you believe.

1. If you were in the crowd would you have gone with Blondin?

....

2. What steps can Christians take to act upon their belief?

....

3. Why is it oftentimes difficult to trust and obey Christ?

....

TEAM EFFORT—HIGH SCHOOL (15-20 MINUTES)

WHAT WOULD YOU DO?

- Divide students into groups of three or four.
- Give each student a copy of "What Would You Do?" on page 123 and a pen or pencil, or display a copy using an overhead projector.
- Students complete the page.

IN THE WORD (25-30 MINUTES)

OBEDIENCE

- Divide students into groups of three or four.
- Give each student a copy of "Obedience" on page 125 and a pen or pencil, or display a copy using an overhead projector.
- Students complete the Bible study.

Andrew Murray put it best: "The starting point and the goal of our Christian life is obedience." If there is a secret to living the Christian life, it is found through obedience.

1. Through our obedience comes freedom and fulfillment. Read John 14:21.
   a. If we say we love God, what will be the result according to this verse?
   (We will obey God's commands.)
   b. Why is this such an important principle in our Christian lives?

2. Jesus is our example of obedience. Read Philippians 2:5-11.
   a. What attitude did Jesus have according to this Scripture?
   (Jesus had humility and obedience.)
   b. What was the result of Jesus' obedience?
   (He died, rose again and brought glory to God.)
   c. What can we do as a group to help one another live a more obedient Christian lifestyle?

1. The checker at the grocery store gives you $.20 too much change. What would you do? How about $2.00, $20.00, $200.00?

....

2. You are not allowed to date a certain person. You go to the mall and there is your special friend and she/he invites you to go get something to eat together. What would you do?

....

3. Your parents won't let you watch a certain movie on television. You go to your friend's house where his/her family invites you to stay, specifically to watch the movie your parents said you couldn't watch. What would you do?

....

4. You are at the store with a friend and your friend sticks a candy bar in your pocket and one in his/hers and then walks out of the store. What would you do?

....

5. Your uncle offers you a glass of wine at a family wedding. You know it's against the law to drink under age but he still hands you a glass. What would you do?

....

WARM UP

A TRIP TO MARS

Imagine for a moment that you have been offered an all-expense paid trip on the first spaceship to the planet Mars. It's just been discovered that there is life on this planet, and people your age. **List five personal items you would take on your trip.**

1. ....
....

2. ....
....

3. ....
....

4. ....
....

5. ....
....
....

Now share why you would choose these items.

....
....
....

TEAM EFFORT

BLONDIN[1]

Before ten thousand screaming people (he) inched his way from the Canadian side of the falls to the United States side. When he got there the crowd began shouting his name: "Blondin! Blondin! Blondin! Blondin!"

Finally he raised his arms, quieted the crowd, and (how's this for an ego trip?) shouted to them, "I am Blondin! Do you believe in me?" the crowd shouted back, "We believe! We believe! We believe!"

Again he quieted the crowd, and once more he shouted to them, "I'm going back across the tightrope, but this time I'm going to carry someone on my back. Do you believe I can do that?" The crowd went dead. Nothing.

Finally out of the crowd stepped one man. He climbed on Blondin's shoulders, and for the next three-and-a-half-hours, Blondin inched his way back across the tightrope to the Canadian side of the falls.

The point of the story is blatantly clear: Ten thousand people stood there that day chanting, "We believe, we believe!" but only one person really believed! Believing is not just saying, "I accept the fact." Believing is giving your life over into the hands of the one in whom you say you believe.

1. If you were in the crowd would you have gone with Blondin?

....

....

....

2. What steps can Christians take to act upon their belief?

....

....

....

3. Why is it oftentimes difficult to trust and obey Christ?

....

....

....

Note

1. Tony Campolo, *You Can Make a Difference* (Waco, TX: Word, 1984), p. 14. Used by permission.

TEAM EFFORT

WHAT WOULD YOU DO?

1. The checker at the grocery store gives you $.20 too much change. What would you do? How about $2.00, $20.00, $200.00? How about $.50 too little change?

....

....

....

2. You are not allowed to date a certain person. You go to the mall and there is your special friend and she/he invites you to go get something to eat together. What would you do?

....

....

....

3. Your parents won't let you watch a certain movie on television. You go to your friend's house where his/her family invites you to stay, specifically to watch the movie your parents said you couldn't watch. What would you do?

....

....

....

4. You are at the store with a friend and your friend sticks a candy bar in your pocket and one in his/hers and then walks out of the store. What would you do?

....

....

....

5. Your uncle offers you a glass of wine at a family wedding. You know it's against the law to drink under age but he still hands you a glass. What would you do?

....

....

IN THE WORD

OBEDIENCE

Andrew Murray put it best: "The starting point and the goal of our Christian life is obedience."
If there is a secret to living the Christian life, it is found through obedience.

1. Through our obedience comes freedom and fulfillment. Read John 14:21.
   a. If we say we love God, what will be the result according to this verse?

   ....

   ....

   ....

   b. Why is this such an important principle in our Christian lives?

   ....

   ....

   ....

2. Jesus is our example of obedience. Read Philippians 2:5-11.
   a. What attitude did Jesus have according to this Scripture?

   ....

   ....

   ....

   b. What was the result of Jesus' obedience?

   ....

   ....

   ....

   c. What can we do as a group to help one another live a more obedient Christian lifestyle?

   ....

   ....

   ....

3. Listed below are several words. With the previous Scriptures in mind, read the word and then discuss how
   obedience to God fits in with each area of our lives.

Servanthood	Boyfriend/Girlfriend
Parents	Parties
Sexuality	Worship
Grades	War

 **So WHAT?**

1. Take a few moments to list areas of your life in which God is calling you to obedience.

....
....
....

2. How will you show obedience to God in these areas?

....
....
....

*T*HINGS TO THINK ABOUT

1. How do you think the standards of our society influence our obedience to God?

....

....

....

2. God loves you! He wants the best for you! How do you think He feels when you walk away from Him in disobedience? How would you feel if you had children who were disobedient to you as a parent?

....

....

....

3. John Calvin wrote, "True knowledge of God is born out of obedience." What do you think about this statement?

....

....

....

PARENT PAGE

OBEDIENCE

Discuss these statements below and how they relate to obedience to God.

1. "But Samuel replied: 'Does the Lord delight in burnt offerings and sacrifices as much as in obeying the voice of the Lord? To obey is better than sacrifice, and to heed is better than the fat of rams'" (1 Samuel 15:22).

2. "True knowledge of God is born out of obedience."—John Calvin

3. "We no longer need to be obedient to our parents or our government. They left us hanging out to dry."
   —17-year-old student, Hoover High School, Glendale, California

4. "The starting point and the goal of our Christian life is obedience."—Andrew Murray

5. "If it feels good do it."—MTV 1994

6. "And this is love: that we walk in obedience to his commands. As you have heard from the beginning, his command is that you walk in love" (2 John 6).

Session 6 "Obedience" Date ....

FAITH

KEY VERSE

"**N**ow faith is being sure of what we hope for and certain of what we do not see." Hebrews 11:1

BIBLICAL BASIS

Matthew 14:22-33;
Mark 10:13-16;
Hebrews 11:1;
James 1:6-8

THE BIG IDEA

God will help us develop our faith and step out in faith.

AIMS OF THIS SESSION

During this session you will guide students to:
• Examine biblical principles of faith;
• Discover practical steps to developing a more childlike faith;
• Implement a decision to step out of their comfort zones and live lives of faith in Christ.

WARM UP

A Day in the Life—
An active melodrama.

TEAM EFFORT— JUNIOR HIGH/ MIDDLE SCHOOL

An Inspiring Story of Faith—
Students examine an example of faith.

TEAM EFFORT— HIGH SCHOOL

Faith Inventory—
Students determine their levels of faith.

IN THE WORD

Childlike Faith—
A Bible study on the faith of children and putting it into action.

THINGS TO THINK ABOUT (OPTIONAL)

Questions to get students thinking and talking about childlike faith.

PARENT PAGE

A tool to get the session into the home and allow parents and young people to discuss faith and doubt.

LEADER'S DEVOTIONAL

"'I don't understand why things can't go back to normal at the end of the half-hour, like The Brady Bunch,' one of the kids remarks as a new mini-crisis takes its place beside the last one nobody quite solved. 'Because,' someone replies, 'Mr. Brady died of AIDS.'"—*Time* review of the film "Reality Bites"

For some strange reason, television has developed a false sense of reality by helping millions of Americans to believe that at the end of a 30-minute show, everything in life will work out fine. Too many people have put their faith in a false hope of a TV reality that doesn't exist. Who would have ever thought the stability of the Brady family would be shattered by AIDS? Reality has a harsh way of challenging the things in which we place our faith.

God's Word says that placing your faith in Jesus Christ develops a firm foundation for your life. How many people or things in society promise a firmer foundation than that of Christ?

A strong faith in Christ grounds you in the reality of God's love. Faith in God offers you peace and hope in the middle of your personal storms. Faith in God is a free gift designed to help you become all that God desires you to be.

Since faith is an intangible sort of word that can confuse young people, this lesson is filled with tangible examples of people who put their faith and trust in God. Anticipate questions from young people who want to know how your faith in Christ makes a difference in your life. Unlike The Brady Bunch, God never promises that we'll have problem-free lives when we put our faith in Christ. God promises that faith in Christ will help us to experience the reality of His love and presence in our lives. (Written by Joey O'Connor.)

SESSION SEVEN · BIBLE TUCK-IN™

FAITH

KEY VERSE

"Now faith is being sure of what we hope for and certain of what we do not see." Hebrews 11:1

BIBLICAL BASIS

Matthew 14:22-33; Mark 10:13-16; Hebrews 11:1; James 1:6-8

THE BIG IDEA

God will help us develop our faith and step out in faith.

WARM UP (10-15 MINUTES)
A DAY IN THE LIFE

• Assign melodrama roles.
• Give each character a copy of "A Day in the Life" on page 137.
• As the narrator reads melodrama, characters perform actions.
• The characters:

1. Manuel—dressed in black	7 and 8. Hours
2. Maggie—the fair maiden	9. Sun
3. Patrick—dressed in white	10. Night
4. Zingerella—the housekeeper	11. Narrator
5 and 6. Curtains	

• Props needed:
Pitcher of water, notes, podium, chalk, trading or postage stamps, broom, pail, banana peel, police whistle, iron, rope, two salt shakers and large wooden match.
• Signs needed:
Curtains (two), Stairs, Time, No (about 30), Hours (two), Sun and Night.

TEAM EFFORT—JUNIOR HIGH/ MIDDLE SCHOOL (15-20 MINUTES)
AN INSPIRING STORY OF FAITH

• Give each student a copy of "An Inspiring Story of Faith" on page 139 and a pen or pencil.
• Read aloud the story.
• Students answer questions.
• As a whole group, discuss the students' responses.

- Fold -

5. Write your own definition of faith.

SO WHAT?

Stepping Out in Faith

Immediately Jesus made the disciples get into the boat and go on ahead of him to the other side, while he dismissed the crowd. After he had dismissed them, he went up on a mountainside by himself to pray. When evening came, he was there alone, but the boat was already a considerable distance from land, buffeted by the waves because the wind was against it.

During the fourth watch of the night Jesus went out to them, walking on the lake. When the disciples saw him walking on the lake, they were terrified.

"It's a ghost," they said, and cried out in fear.

But Jesus immediately said to them: "Take courage! It is I. Don't be afraid."

"Lord, if it's you," Peter replied, "tell me to come to you on the water."

"Come," he said.

Then Peter got down out of the boat, walked on the water and came toward Jesus. But when he saw the wind, he was afraid and, beginning to sink, cried out, "Lord, save me!"

Immediately Jesus reached out his hand and caught him. "You of little faith," he said, "why did you doubt?"

And when they climbed into the boat, the wind died down. Then those who were in the boat worshiped him, saying, "Truly you are the Son of God" (Matthew 14:22-33).

1. If I had been Peter and Jesus invited me to step out in faith from the boat to the water, I probably would have:

2. When it comes to stepping out in faith:

☐ Struggle with doubts ☐ Am often afraid
☐ Have a go-for-it attitude ☐ Very tentatively do it
☐ Gripe about it ☐ Wait for someone else and then follow
☐ Other

3. In what area(s) of your life is God calling you to step out in faith?

4. What is holding you back from making this commitment to jump in the water with Jesus?
Here's a checklist for stepping out in faith:
☐ Will it glorify God?
☐ Is it biblical?
☐ How do the significant people in my life feel about it?
☐ Do I sense God's leading?

THINGS TO THINK ABOUT (OPTIONAL)

• Use the questions on page 147 after or as a part of "In the Word."

1. Why do you think it is often easier for children than adolescents or adults to have faith?

2. Why is childlike faith difficult at times?

3. Who in your life is an example of childlike faith?

PARENT PAGE

• Distribute page to parents.

Things looked bleak for the children in George Muller's orphanage at Ashley Downs in England. It was time for breakfast, and there was no food. A small girl whose father was a close friend of Muller's was visiting in the orphanage. Muller took her hand and said, "Come and see what our heavenly Father will do."

In the dining room, long tables were set with empty plates and empty mugs. Not only was there no food in the kitchen, but there was no money in the orphanage's account. Muller prayed, "Dear Father, we thank you for what you are going to give us to eat."

Immediately, they heard a knock at the door. When they opened it, there stood the local baker. "Mr. Muller," he said, "I couldn't sleep last night. Somehow I felt you had no bread for breakfast, so I got up at two o'clock and baked fresh bread. Here it is." Muller thanked him and gave praise to God.

Soon, a second knock was heard. It was the milkman. His cart had broken down in the front of the orphanage. He said he would like to give the children the milk so he could empty the cart and repair it.

1. What does this story tell you about George Muller?

2. How is this like or unlike your experience with prayer?

3. What steps can we take in our lives to have a stronger faith?

TEAM EFFORT—HIGH SCHOOL (15-20 MINUTES)

FAITH INVENTORY

• Give each student a copy of "Faith Inventory" on page 141 and a pen or pencil.
• Students individually complete survey.
• Divide students into groups of three or four.
• Students complete questions.

Above each statement is a continuum from 1 to 10 (1 = total unbelief and 10 = total belief). Circle a number to show where your faith is on each statement.

There is a God.
1 2 3 4 5 6 7 8 9 10

God loves me.
1 2 3 4 5 6 7 8 9 10

Jesus is God.
1 2 3 4 5 6 7 8 9 10

Jesus rose from the dead.
1 2 3 4 5 6 7 8 9 10

God answers prayer.
1 2 3 4 5 6 7 8 9 10

The Bible is true.
1 2 3 4 5 6 7 8 9 10

- - - - - - - - - Fold - - - - - - - - -

IN THE WORD (20-25 MINUTES)

CHILDLIKE FAITH

• Invite a panel of 4- and 5-year-olds to your group. Have your students ask them questions about God. Some questions to help fuel the fire could be: Where does God live? How big is God? Does God ever talk to you? What does God look like? Did Jesus live in America? Do you love God? Does God listen to your prayers?
• Give each student a copy of "Childlike Faith" on page 143 and a pen or pencil, or display a copy using an overhead projector.
• Divide students into groups of three or four.
• Students complete the Bible study.
Read Mark 10:13-16.

1. Why do you think Jesus' own disciples didn't want the children to come to Him? (They didn't think Jesus would want to bother with children.)

2. What point was Jesus making to His disciples when He rebuked them? (Children offer them a good example of how they should be.)

3. When you picture Jesus (verse 16) blessing the little children, what comes to your mind? Some of the special qualities of a child are:
- Trusting
- Sense of wonder
- Forgiving
- Total dependence
- Frank openness
- Complete sincerity

4. How do these traits relate to faith in God? (These traits need to be a part of our faith in God.) Next to each of the traits above, put a number from 1 to 10 (1 = needs vast improvement and 10 = I've got this trait down pat) as the trait relates to your faith in God. "Now faith is being sure of what we hope for and certain of what we do not see" (Hebrews 11:1).

1. What is your definition of faith?

2. What is your definition of doubt?

There is a heaven.
1 2 3 4 5 6 7 8 9 10

God is in control of the universe.
1 2 3 4 5 6 7 8 9 10

God wants the best for my life.
1 2 3 4 5 6 7 8 9 10

God forgives me of confessed sins.
1 2 3 4 5 6 7 8 9 10

WARM UP

A DAY IN THE LIFE

The characters

1. Manuel—dressed in black	7 and 8. Hours
2. Maggie—the fair maiden	9. Sun
3. Patrick—dressed in white	10. Night
4. Zingerella—the housekeeper	11. Narrator
5 and 6. Curtains	

The curtains part. (Two people holding "Curtains" signs stand at center stage and walk away from each other.) The sun rises. (Person holding "Sun" sign stands up.) Our play begins.

Manuel de Populo, son of a wealthy merchant, is in his study, carefully pouring over his notes. (He pours water from a pitcher over some notes.) He stamps his feet impatiently (He licks stamps and sticks them on shoes.) and calls for his maid, Zingerella.

Zingerella tears down the stairs (She rips "Stairs" sign.) and trips into the room. (She trips.)

"Go fetch Maggie O'Toole," demands Manuel. Zingerella flies (She waves arms in flying motion.) to do her master's bidding.

Time passes. (Person holding "Time" sign walks across stage.)

Manuel crosses the floor once, twice, thrice. (He uses chalk to draw three big X's on the floor.) At last Maggie comes sweeping into the room. (She sweeps floor with a broom.)

"For the last time, will you marry me?" insists Manuel. Maggie turns a little pale. (She turns a pail upside down.)

"No," she shouts, "a thousand times No." (She throws papers with "No" on them.)

"Then I will have to cast you into the dungeon," says Manuel in a rage. She throws herself at his feet (She falls at his feet and lies there.)

"Oh, Sir," she pleads, "I appeal to you." (She hands him a banana peel.)

Haughtily, he says, "Your appeal is fruitless." (He hands her back the banana peel.) At that, Manuel stomps out of the room. (He stamps his feet.)

Maggie flies about in a dither. (She waves arms in a flying motion.) Oh, if only Patrick would come, he would save her!

The hours pass slowly. (Two people with "Hours" signs walk across the stage.) Finally, Maggie takes her stand (She stands behind podium.) and scans the horizon. (She puts hand above eyes in a a searching motion.) Suddenly she hears a whistle. (Patrick blows a whistle.) Could it be???

"Maggie, it is I, my love, your Patrick!!!"

He enters the room and tenderly presses her hand. (He irons her hand with an iron.) She throws him a line. (She throws a rope at him.) Just at that moment, Manuel re-enters and challenges Patrick to a duel. In a fury, they assault each other. (They sprinkle salt on each other.) Finally Manuel gives up the match. (He hands Patrick a match.) and departs.

"At last, you are mine!" says Patrick. He leads his love away into the night. (Person holding "Night" sign falls down.) The sun sets. (Person holding "Sun" sign sits down.) Night falls. (Person holding "Night" sign falls down.) The curtains come together (Two people holding "Curtains" signs walk toward each other.) and our play is ended.

TEAM EFFORT

AN INSPIRING STORY OF FAITH

Things looked bleak for the children in George Muller's orphanage at Ashley Downs in England. It was time for breakfast, and there was no food. A small girl whose father was a close friend of Muller's was visiting in the orphanage. Muller took her hand and said, "Come and see what our heavenly Father will do."

In the dining room, long tables were set with empty plates and empty mugs. Not only was there no food in the kitchen, but there was no money in the orphanage's account. Muller prayed, "Dear Father, we thank you for what you are going to give us to eat."

Immediately, they heard a knock at the door. When they opened it, there stood the local baker. "Mr. Muller," he said, "I couldn't sleep last night. Somehow I felt you had no bread for breakfast, so I got up at two o'clock and baked fresh bread. Here it is." Muller thanked him and gave praise to God.

Soon, a second knock was heard. It was the milkman. His cart had broken down in the front of the orphanage. He said he would like to give the children the milk so he could empty the cart and repair it.

1. What does this story tell you about George Muller?

....

....

....

2. How is this like or unlike your experience with prayer?

....

....

....

3. What steps can we take in our lives to have a stronger faith?

....

....

....

 TEAM EFFORT

FAITH INVENTORY

Above each statement is a continuum from 1 to 10 (1 = total unbelief and 10 = total belief). Circle a number to show where your faith is on each statement.

1	2	3	4	5	6	7	8	9	10

There is a God.

1	2	3	4	5	6	7	8	9	10

God loves me.

1	2	3	4	5	6	7	8	9	10

Jesus is God.

1	2	3	4	5	6	7	8	9	10

Jesus rose from the dead.

1	2	3	4	5	6	7	8	9	10

God answers prayer.

1	2	3	4	5	6	7	8	9	10

The Bible is true.

1	2	3	4	5	6	7	8	9	10

There is a heaven.

1	2	3	4	5	6	7	8	9	10

God is in control of the universe.

1	2	3	4	5	6	7	8	9	10

God wants the best for my life.

1	2	3	4	5	6	7	8	9	10

God forgives me of confessed sins.

1. What is your definition of faith?

....

....

....

....

2. What is your definition of doubt?

....

....

....

....

IN THE WORD

CHILDLIKE FAITH

Read Mark 10:13-16.

1. Why do you think Jesus' own disciples didn't want the children to come to Him?

....

....

....

2. What point was Jesus making to His disciples when He rebuked them?

....

....

....

3. When you picture Jesus (v. 16) blessing the little children, what comes to your mind?

....

....

Some of the special qualities of a child are:

• Trusting
• Sense of wonder
• Forgiving
• Total dependence
• Frank openness
• Complete sincerity

4. How do these traits relate to faith in God?

....

....

Next to each of the traits above, put a number from 1 to 10 (1 = needs vast improvement and 10 = I've got this trait down pat) as the trait relates to your faith in God.

"Now faith is being sure of what we hope for and certain of what we do not see" (Hebrews 11:1).

5. Write your own definition of faith.

....

....

....

So WHAT?

Stepping Out in Faith

Immediately Jesus made the disciples get into the boat and go on ahead of him to the other side, while he dismissed the crowd. After he had dismissed them, he went up on a mountainside by himself to pray. When evening came, he was there alone, but the boat was already a considerable distance from land, buffeted by the waves because the wind was against it.

During the fourth watch of the night Jesus went out to them, walking on the lake. When the disciples saw him walking on the lake, they were terrified.

"It's a ghost," they said, and cried out in fear.

But Jesus immediately said to them: "Take courage! It is I. Don't be afraid."

"Lord, if it's you," Peter replied, "tell me to come to you on the water."

"Come," he said.

Then Peter got down out of the boat, walked on the water and came toward Jesus. But when he saw the wind, he was afraid and, beginning to sink, cried out, "Lord, save me!"

Immediately Jesus reached out his hand and caught him. "You of little faith," he said, "why did you doubt?"

And when they climbed into the boat, the wind died down. Then those who were in the boat worshiped him, saying, "Truly you are the Son of God" (Matthew 14:22-33).

1. If I had been Peter and Jesus invited me to step out in faith from the boat to the water, I probably would have:

....

....

2. When it comes to stepping out in faith I:
- ☐ Struggle with doubts
- ☐ Am often afraid
- ☐ Have a go-for-it attitude
- ☐ Very tentatively do it
- ☐ Gripe about it
- ☐ Wait for someone else and then follow
- ☐ Other _____

3. In what area(s) of your life is God calling you to step out in faith?

....

....

....

4. What is holding you back from making this commitment to jump in the water with Jesus?

....

....

Here's a checklist for stepping out in faith:
- ☐ Will it glorify God?
- ☐ Is it biblical?
- ☐ How do the significant people in my life feel about it?
- ☐ Do I sense God's leading?

FAITH

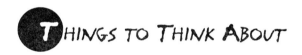

THINGS TO THINK ABOUT

1. Why do you think it is often easier for children than adolescents or adults to have faith?

....

....

....

2. Why is childlike faith difficult at times?

....

....

....

3. Who in your life is an example of childlike faith?

....

....

....

FAITH

PARENT PAGE

FAITH AND DOUBT

Circle *T* for true or *F* for false and then discuss your answers.

T or F   Faith can be intellectual suicide.

T or F   Doubt is a necessary part of faith.

T or F   When in doubt, feed your faith and you'll starve your doubts to death.

T or F   Christianity is not true because it works, it is true because it's true.

T or F   Faith is the opposite of doubt.

T or F   Sometimes doubt comes from a faulty view of God.

T or F   Some Christians have weak foundations because they don't know what they believe.

T or F   Doubts always occur during times of lack of commitment.

Read James 1:6-8.

1. How is the person of doubt described in this section of Scripture?

....

....

....

2. How can we keep from being a person like the person described in this passage?

....

....

Since doubt is a natural part of the spiritual life, we need help in combating our doubts. Here is a list of suggestions on how to handle your doubts. Circle the ones that are most significant for you and share them with your family.

1. Don't panic when a doubt arrives.

2. Be honest about it. Work it out–don't ignore it.

3. Stay in fellowship–don't drop out.

4. Seek God more through reading the Bible and prayer.

5. Don't be afraid to think new thoughts and test new avenues of faith.

6. Remember, faith is a mystery.

7. Continued, unconfessed sin can bring doubt into our lives. Ask God to forgive sins that are troubling you.

8. Learn to doubt your doubt.

Session 7 "Faith" Date ....

SPIRITUAL GROWTH

KEY VERSE

"Being confident of this, that he who began a good work in you will carry it on to completion until the day of Christ Jesus." Philippians 1:6

BIBLICAL BASIS

Philippians 1:6;
Colossians 3:1-17

THE BIG IDEA

Spiritual growth is not stagnant but, through the ups and downs of life, is always moving toward a closer walk with God.

AIMS OF THIS SESSION

During this session you will guide students to:
• Examine biblical principles of spiritual growth;
• Discover key ways to develop a more godly lifestyle and deeper relationship with Christ;
• Implement practical decisions to grow spiritually.

WARM UP

I...—
Students share their ideas and wishes.

TEAM EFFORT— JUNIOR HIGH/ MIDDLE SCHOOL

Personal Growth Check List—
Students inventory their spiritual lives.

TEAM EFFORT— HIGH SCHOOL

Footprints—
A story illustrating God's part in our growth.

IN THE WORD

Growing Toward God—
A Bible study on how to grow spiritually.

THINGS TO THINK ABOUT (OPTIONAL)

Questions to get students thinking and talking about growing spiritually.

PARENT PAGE

A tool to get the session into the home and allow parents and young people to discuss how they grow spiritually.

LEADER'S DEVOTIONAL

"I don't pig out. I basically eat everything I want; I've just changed what it is I want to eat."—Oprah Winfrey

Eat right and exercise. It's the time-tested, simple prescription for good health. Everyone knows eating right and exercising regularly will promote health, but how many people really practice what they already know to be true? That's where Oprah can help us out. Everyone with an inquiring mind has known about her weight struggles. Listen to her words again, "I basically eat everything I want; I've just changed what it is I want to eat."

Attitude. It makes a big difference in dieting and physical fitness. And a good attitude makes a tremendous difference in spiritual growth. Just like no one can make you healthy, no one can make you grow in your relationship with God. Spiritual growth is an intentional process to develop your friendship with Jesus Christ. A balanced diet of digesting God's Word and exercising your faith in everyday life will help you grow as a Christian. There are all sorts of temptations to divert your attention away from God. But when you change your desires to God's desires, you'll be able to grow strong in your walk with Christ. The Bible says not to indulge your flesh nature, but to hunger for the things of God. Growth in Christ comes from planting and cultivating the fruit of God's Spirit. By feeding on God's Word, you'll have all the strength you need to put it into practice.

This lesson offers all sorts of practical tools to help students understand spiritual growth. As you grow in your relationship with God this week, ask God to give you a deep desire and hunger for His Word. The young people you minister to will give you plenty of opportunities to exercise your faith in Christ. (Written by Joey O'Connor.)

S E S S I O N   E I G H T   **B I B L E   T U C K - I N** ™

SPIRITUAL GROWTH

 KEY VERSE

"Being confident of this, that he who began a good work in you will carry it on to completion until the day of Christ Jesus." Philippians 1:6

B IBLICAL BASIS

Philippians 1:6; Colossians 3:1-17

T HE BIG IDEA

Spiritual growth is not stagnant but, through the ups and downs of life, is always moving toward a closer walk with God.

W ARM UP (5-10 Minutes)

I...

• Give each student a copy of "I..." on page 155 and a pen or pencil.

• Students complete the page.
Complete each statement.

I plan to change...

....

I enjoy...

....

I wish...

....

I can hardly believe...

....

I will always...

....

-------------------------- Fold --------------------------

---

2. Write a plan for how you will specifically work on that attribute.

....

T HINGS TO THINK ABOUT (OPTIONAL)

• Use the questions on page 163 after or as a part of "In the Word."

1. What is the difference between salvation and spiritual growth?

....

2. How does Philippians 1:6 relate to spiritual growth?

....

3. If someone is feeling dry spiritually and they say they feel far from God, what advice would you give them?

....

P ARENT PAGE

• Distribute page to parents.

PERSONAL GROWTH CHECK LIST

- Give each student a copy of "Personal Growth Check List" on page 157 and a pen or pencil.
- Students complete the page.

On the left-hand side, rank order (1 = most important to 10 = least important) the following areas of spiritual growth.

.... Daily quiet time with God
.... Sharing your faith with others
.... Giving money to the church
.... Helping those in need
.... Attending worship service
.... Telling the truth
.... Obedience to parents
.... Not being anxious or worrying
.... Fellowship with other Christians
.... Being a member of a church
.... Prayer

Now on the right-hand side, rank order (1=excellent to 10=poorly) how you are doing in each of these areas.

What areas of spiritual growth can you work on this week?

TEAM EFFORT—HIGH SCHOOL (15-20 MINUTES)

FOOTPRINTS

- Give each student a copy of "Footprints" on page 159 and a pen or pencil.
- Read aloud the story.
- As a whole group, discuss the students' responses.

One night a man had a dream. He dreamed he was walking along the beach with the Lord. Across the sky flashed scenes from his life. For each scene, he noticed two sets of footprints in the sand; one belonged to him and the other to the Lord.

When the last scene of his life flashed before him, he looked back at the footprints in the sand. He noticed that many times along the path of his life there was only one set of footprints. He also noticed that it happened at the very lowest and saddest times in his life.

This really bothered him and he questioned the Lord about it: "Lord, You said that once I decided to follow You, You'd walk with me all the way. But I have noticed that during the most troublesome times in my life, there is only one set of footprints. I don't understand why when I needed You most You would leave me."

The Lord replied, "My precious, precious child, I love you and would never leave you. During your times of trial and suffering, when you see only one set of footprints, it was then that I carried you."

Now create a two-year spiritual growth chart. Chart out some of your ups and downs. Then discuss these questions.

JANUARY   JULY   DECEMBER

JANUARY   JULY   DECEMBER

JANUARY   JULY   DECEMBER

1. Where and when was God especially close?

2. Where and when did He seem far away?

3. What causes growth in our spiritual lives?

4. Is there anything wrong with a chart that looks like a roller coaster?

5. How can even the difficult times be times of growth?

IN THE WORD (25-30 MINUTES)

GROWING TOWARD GOD

- Divide students into groups of three or four.
- Give each student a copy of "Growing Toward God" on page 161 and a pen or pencil.
- Students complete page.

1. What spiritual growth principles can you find together in this powerful passage? Read Colossians 3:1-17.

2. List the attributes of a new nature found in verses 12-17. (Compassion, kindness, humility, gentleness, patience, bear with each other, forgive each other, love, have peace in your heart.)

3. How did Jesus model these attributes?

Next to each, list how you could live out that attribute at your school. Now list how you could live out that attribute in your home. "And whatever you do, whether in word or in deed, do it all in the name of the Lord Jesus, giving thanks to God the Father through him" (Colossians 3:17).

4. What does it mean to "do it all in the name of the Lord Jesus"?

SO WHAT?

1. Put a mark by each attribute of the new nature that you desire to work on this week.

Fold

WARM UP

I...

Complete each statement.

I plan to change... ....

....

I enjoy... ....

....

I wish... ....

....

I can hardly believe... ....

....

I will always... ....

....

TEAM EFFORT

PERSONAL GROWTH CHECK LIST

On the left-hand side, rank order (1 = most important to 10 = least important) the following areas of spiritual growth.

....	Daily quiet time with God	....
....	Sharing your faith with others	....
....	Giving money to the church	....
....	Helping those in need	....
....	Attending worship service	....
....	Telling the truth	....
....	Obedience to parents	....
....	Not being anxious or worrying	....
....	Fellowship with other Christians	....
....	Being a member of a church	....
....	Prayer	....

Now on the right-hand side, rank order (1=excellent to 10=poorly) how you are doing in each of these areas.

What areas of spiritual growth can you work on this week?

....

....

....

TEAM EFFORT

FOOTPRINTS[1]

One night a man had a dream. He dreamed he was walking along the beach with the Lord. Across the sky flashed scenes from his life. For each scene, he noticed two sets of footprints in the sand; one belonged to him and the other to the Lord.

When the last scene of his life flashed before him, he looked back at the footprints in the sand. He noticed that many times along the path of his life there was only one set of footprints. He also noticed that it happened at the very lowest and saddest times in his life.

This really bothered him and he questioned the Lord about it: "Lord, You said that once I decided to follow You, You'd walk with me all the way. But I have noticed that during the most troublesome times in my life, there is only one set of footprints. I don't understand why when I needed You most You would leave me."

The Lord replied, "My precious, precious child. I love you and would never leave you. During your times of trial and suffering, when you see only one set of footprints, it was then that I carried you."

Now create a two-year spiritual growth chart. Chart out some of your ups and downs. Then discuss these questions.

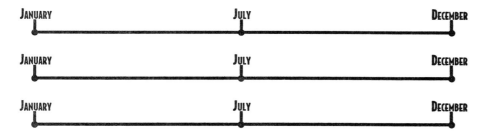

1. Where and when was God especially close?

2. Where and when did He seem far away?

3. What causes growth in our spiritual lives?

4. Is there anything wrong with a chart that looks like a roller coaster?

5. How can even the difficult times be times of growth?

Note

1. Author unknown.

SPIRITUAL GROWTH

IN THE WORD

GROWING TOWARD GOD

Read Colossians 3:1-17.

1. What spiritual growth principles can you find together in this powerful passage?

....

....

....

2. List the attributes of a new nature found in verses 12-17.

....

....

....

3. How did Jesus model these attributes?

....

....

Next to each, list how you could live out that attribute at your school.

Now list how you could live out that attribute in your home.

"And whatever you do, whether in word or in deed, do it all in the name of the Lord Jesus, giving thanks to God the Father through him" (Colossians 3:17).

4. What does it mean to "do it all in the name of the Lord Jesus"?

....

....

SO WHAT?

1. Put a mark by each attribute of the new nature that you desire to work on this week.

....

....

2. Write a plan for how you will specifically work on that attribute.

....

....

THINGS TO THINK ABOUT

1. What is the difference between salvation and spiritual growth?

....

....

....

2. How does Philippians 1:6 relate to spiritual growth?

....

....

....

3. If someone is feeling dry spiritually and they say they feel far from God, what advice would you give them?

....

....

....

SPIRITUAL GROWTH

 **P**ARENT **P**AGE

THE **S**PIRITUAL **G**ROWTH **I**NTERVIEW
Interview each other using the following questions.

1. When was the first time you remember God being present in your life?

....

....

....

2. When has God sustained you through a difficult time?

....

....

....

3. Who has been a major spiritual influence in your life?

....

....

....

4. Do you have a favorite verse or Bible story? If yes, what is it?

....

....

....

5. If you could ask God one question about spiritual growth, what would you ask?

....

....

....

Session 8 "Spiritual Growth" Date ....

GOD'S WILL

LEADER'S PEP TALK

One of my modern-day heroes is Terry Foxe. Terry was a Canadian runner who attempted to run the entire distance from the east coast of Canada to Vancouver, British Columbia, in order to raise money for cancer research. Terry knew the needs of cancer victims intimately because he was one himself—he was running across Canada with an artificial leg. This amputee ran 26 miles every day, six days a week, to raise money for cancer.

Terry's enthusiasm and zeal for life caught my attention during his run, and I remember, day after day, seeing him on the news. People, mainly children, would be gathering around him and he would usually be standing in front of a microphone in a park or shopping center or church building. He would often say, "I don't know about tomorrow, but I'm thankful for today, and I'm going to make the most of this one day God has given me. I'm going to live one day at a time." I'm not even sure Terry knew he was quoting Jesus in Matthew 6:34.

I think Jesus summed up doing the will of God in two simple verses:

> But seek first his kingdom and his righteousness, and all these things will be given to you as well. Therefore do not worry about tomorrow, for tomorrow will worry about itself: Each day has enough trouble of its own (Matthew 6:33,34).

In this section you will have the privilege of helping your students better understand God's will for their lives and how He reveals it through Jesus, the Holy Spirit and the Church. Two of the most often asked questions I receive from kids are "How do I know the will of God?" and "How can I be absolutely sure she/he is the one for me?" Actually I think we've been asking the wrong questions. Understanding the will of God is probably closer to the Scripture above: 1. seek Him first, and 2. then follow Him one day at a time.

Thanks again for your involvement in kids' lives. This little poem was written by another twentieth-century hero of mine named Sam Shoemaker. He pretty much sums up your important job of working with kids.

I stand by the door.
I neither go too far in, nor stay out.
The door is the most important in the world—
It is the door through which men walk when they find God.
There's no use my going way inside, and staying there,
When so many are still outside and they, as much as I,
Crave to know where the door is.
And all that so many ever find,
Is only the wall where the door ought to be.
They creep along the wall like blind men,
With outstretched, groping hands.
Feeling for a door, knowing there must be a door,
Yet never find it...
So I stand by the door.
The most tremendous thing in the world,
Is for men to find that door—the door of God.

THE WILL OF GOD

KEY VERSE

"Delight yourself in the Lord and he will give you the desires of your heart." Psalm 37:4

BIBLICAL BASIS

Exodus 20:12,14,15;
Psalm 37:4; 119:105;
Proverbs 3:5,6; 11:14; 16:9; 20:18;
Matthew 6:25-34; 22:37;
Romans 12:1,2;
1 Corinthians 6:19,20;
Philippians 4:6,7;
Colossians 3:1-4;
James 1:5-8,26

THE BIG IDEA

The Scripture is filled with God's will for our lives. As we follow Him daily, He will provide guidance and direction because He loves us.

AIMS OF THIS SESSION

During this session you will guide students to:
• Examine the principles for knowing God's will for their lives;
• Discover the different ways God presents His will for their lives;
• Commit themselves to God's will for their lives.

WARM UP

I Am—
Students share who they are.

TEAM EFFORT— JUNIOR HIGH/ MIDDLE SCHOOL

The Will of God Quiz—
A look at what the will of God is.

TEAM EFFORT— HIGH SCHOOL

Who's Responsible?—
Students determine their part in God's will.

IN THE WORD

Road Signs to Finding the Will of God—
A Bible study on knowing God's will.

THINGS TO THINK ABOUT (OPTIONAL)

Questions to get students thinking and talking about how to live in God's will.

PARENT PAGE

A tool to get the session into the home and allow parents and young people to discuss trusting in God's will.

LEADER'S DEVOTIONAL

"'Believing that true love waits, I make a commitment to God, myself, my family, those I date, my future mate and my children to be sexually pure until the day I enter marriage.' What does it all mean? Perhaps that 30 years after the steamy outbreak of the sexual revolution—and in a country where 40 percent of our ninth graders say they have already had sex—at least some American adolescents are looking for a little less heat. And believing, with the enthusiasm of youth, that less heat may somehow generate more light."—*Life*, September 1994

When over 200,000 teenagers pledge to wait to be sexually active until marriage, it's clear that knowing the will of God can make dramatic changes in young people's lives. Not only will the True Love Waits campaign change millions of young people's lives worldwide, it will be a powerful testimony to all believers in how to live out the will of God expressed in His Word.

Young people, like many adults, spend a lot of time wondering about God's will for their decisions, future, dating and circumstances. "What does God think?" "Does He have all the control or do I have the power to make my own decisions?" "How can I know God's will?" This lesson will help students know that God's will can be known and practiced in a way that makes powerful changes in their lives.

The important thing not to miss while searching for the will of God is God Himself. People can spend their lives seeking to discover God's will for each and every situation, but miss the wonderful opportunity to know their Creator! God created you to have fellowship with Him. He gave you His Word as a foundation and guide for your life. Just like a map won't decide for you whether to take the freeway or the highway, God's Word is designed to help you make wise decisions as you journey through life. It's written to help you know and experience a meaningful relationship with God through Jesus Christ. God's Holy Spirit will lead, guide, nudge, protect and provide you with the wisdom to make decisions to honor God.

As you prepare this lesson, spend some time reflecting on God's will for your life. How much time do you spend wondering what God's will is? Do you seek to live out what you already know of His will as given in His Word? How can we focus on knowing God personally instead of constantly looking for specific answers to questions? Knowing God's will for our lives overflows from first knowing God Himself. Just ask the 211,163 teenagers who are willing to wait for sex until marriage. (Written by Joey O'Connor.)

BIBLE *TUCK-IN*™

THE WILL OF GOD

KEY VERSE

"Delight yourself in the Lord and he will give you the desires of your heart." Psalm 37:4

BIBLICAL BASIS

Exodus 20:12,14,15; Psalm 37:4; 119:105; Proverbs 3:5,6; 11:14; 16:9; 20:18; Matthew 6:25-34; 22:37; Romans 12:1,2; 1 Corinthians 6:19,20; Philippians 4:6,7; Colossians 3:1-4; James 1:5-8,26

THE BIG IDEA

The Scripture is filled with God's will for our lives. As we follow Him daily, He will provide guidance and direction because He loves us.

WARM UP (5-10 Minutes)
I AM

• Give each student a copy of "I Am" on page 173 and a pen or pencil.
• Students complete the page.

List 10 "I am's" and share them with another person. (Example: I am a student, Christian, daughter or son, softball player, etc.)

1. I am
2. I am
3. I am
4. I am
5. I am
6. I am
7. I am
8. I am
9. I am
10. I am

TEAM EFFORT—JUNIOR HIGH/ MIDDLE SCHOOL (15-20 Minutes)

THE WILL OF GOD QUIZ

• Give each student a copy of "The Will of God Quiz" on page 175 and a pen or pencil, or display a copy using an overhead projector.
• Students complete the page individually.
• As a whole group, discuss students' responses.

---

3. Prayer

Prayer is another way of knowing the will of God. James tells us to ask God for wisdom, expecting Him to give it to us generously (see James 1:5-8).

Paul gave strong advice to his friends in the Philippian church when he wrote: "Don't worry about anything; instead, pray about everything; tell God your needs and don't forget to thank him for his answers" (Phil. 4:6, *TLB*).

a. What does Paul suggest you do instead of worrying about God's will?

(Pray and let God know your needs.)

b. Read Philippians 4:7. List the result of following Paul's instructions.

(God will give you His peace.)

c. What are some specific areas in your life that you should be praying about?

4. Circumstances

At times, we can know the will of God through circumstances (see Proverbs 3:5,6; 16:9). Some people call it the open-door/closed-door policy of knowing circumstances. Be careful to look at events and situations over which you have no control as possible actions from God. Watch them carefully and slowly. Don't act impulsively on circumstances. Use the other methods of prayer, Bible reading and the wise counsel of others to help you see if the circumstances are from God.

a. What are a couple of circumstances over which you had no control that you believe God used to lead you to do His will?

b. Now, as a group, ask for volunteers to provide a problem or issue and ask the group to look at each problem or issue according to this road map. (For example: Dating a non-Christian or what church I should attend.)

SO WHAT?

1. Are there any issues in your life you *need/want* to give over to the will of God? List them.

2. Read Romans 12:1,2. How does it relate to your life and the will of God?

THINGS TO THINK ABOUT (OPTIONAL)

• Use the questions on page 185 after or as a part of "In the Word."

1. What does "Delight yourself in the Lord and he will give you the desires of your heart" (Psalm 37:4) mean?

2. Does God have the perfect job, person to marry, etc., picked out for you?

3. Sometimes you make a wrong decision. How does that fit into God's will?

4. Why is it so important to seek the advice of someone you respect?

5. Do you think there is ever more than one option that would fit into God's will?

PARENT PAGE

• Distribute page to parents.

Yes No 1. Has God ever communicated with you directly?
Yes No 2. Does God have an absolute moral standard for man?
Yes No 3. Are people responsible to God for their actions?
Yes No 4. Can two people be led by God to do two contradictory things?
Yes No 5. Has God already chosen a spouse for you?
Yes No 6. If you make a wrong major decision, can you ever be in God's will?
Yes No 7. Have you ever consulted the Bible when making a decision and found help?
Yes No 8. Should God be consulted when selecting a career?
Yes No 9. Should God be consulted when buying clothes?
Yes No 10. Should God be consulted when selecting a deodorant?

TEAM EFFORT—HIGH SCHOOL (15-20 MINUTES)

WHO'S RESPONSIBLE?

- Divide students into groups of three or four.
- Give each student a copy of "Who's Responsible?" on page 177 and a pen or pencil, or display a copy using an overhead projector.
- Students complete the page.
- As a whole group, discuss students' responses.

	Primarily My Responsibility	Primarily God's Responsibility	Too Close To Call
Protecting me from drunk drivers			
Getting an A in class			
My decision to become a Christian			
Keeping me from illness			
Deciding whom I should marry or if I should marry			
Understanding Scripture			
Choosing my life work			
Finances			
Health			
Sexual purity			

172

— — — — — — — — — Fold — — — — — — — — —

IN THE WORD (25-30 MINUTES)

ROAD SIGNS TO FINDING THE WILL OF GOD

- Divide students into groups of three or four.
- Give each student a copy of "Road Signs to Finding the Will of God" on pages 179 to 181 and a pen or pencil, or display a copy using an overhead projector.
- Students complete the Bible study.

1. The Bible

We can know the will of God through the Bible.

"Thy word is a lamp unto my feet, and a light unto my path" (Psalm 119:105, *KJV*).

The Bible is our authority when it comes to knowing God's will. As we read and study the Bible, we can know how God wants us to live in many situations. Look up the following verses and match them to the word or phrase found in the Bible that is God's will for our lives.

Love the Lord your God with all your heart, mind and soul. (Matthew 22:37)		James 1:26
Be thankful in all situations. (1 Thessalonians 5:18)		Matthew 6:33
Do not be conformed to this world. (Romans 12:1,2)		Exodus 20:12
Seek first God's kingdom. (Matthew 6:33)		Exodus 20:14,15
Keep a tight rein on your tongue. (James 1:26)		1 Corinthians
Do not commit adultery or steal. (Exodus 20:14,15) 5:18		1 Thessalonians
Honor your father and mother. (Exodus 20:12)		Romans 12:1,2
Honor God with your body. (1 Corinthians 6:19,20)		Matthew 22:37

2. Counsel

Seek advice and counsel of others whom you respect. We all need to take the advice of the writer of Proverbs seriously. "Make plans by seeking advice" (Proverbs 20:18). "Where there is no guidance, the people fall; but in abundance of counselors there is victory" (Proverbs 11:14, *NASB*). Who can you go to for good, solid, sound advice?

The list could go on and on. However, the Bible does not deal with every situation. For example, nowhere in Scripture will you find what college you should attend, or whether you should drive a VW or Chevrolet. When Scripture is silent on a subject, we look at other indicators to find out the will of God for our lives.

You need people in your life, perhaps in your family or at your church, to whom you can go to for advice and counsel. Weigh their thoughts heavily, but remember, you must ultimately make your own decisions.

THE WILL OF GOD

WARM UP

I AM

List 10 "I am's" and share them with another person. (Example: I am a student, Christian, daughter or son, softball player, etc.)

1. I am ....
2. I am ....
3. I am ....
4. I am ....
5. I am ....
6. I am ....
7. I am ....
8. I am ....
9. I am ....
10. I am ....

TEAM EFFORT

THE WILL OF GOD QUIZ[1]

Yes	No	1.	Has God ever communicated with you directly?
Yes	No	2.	Does God have an absolute moral standard for man?
Yes	No	3.	Are people responsible to God for their actions?
Yes	No	4.	Can two people be led by God to do two contradictory things?
Yes	No	5.	Has God already chosen a spouse for you?
Yes	No	6.	If you make a wrong major decision, can you ever be in God's will?
Yes	No	7.	Have you ever consulted the Bible when making a decision and found help?
Yes	No	8.	Should God be consulted when selecting a career?
Yes	No	9.	Should God be consulted when buying clothes?
Yes	No	10.	Should God be consulted when selecting a deodorant?

Note

1. *Ideas 1-4* (El Cajon, CA: Youth Specialties, 1979), p. 104. Used by permission.

TEAM EFFORT

WHO'S RESPONSIBLE?

	Primarily My Responsibility	Primarily God's Responsibility	Too Close To Call
Protecting me from drunk drivers			
Getting an A in class			
My decision to become a Christian			
Keeping me from illness			
Deciding whom I should marry or if I should marry			
Understanding Scripture			
Choosing my life work			
Finances			
Health			
Sexual purity			

IN THE WORD

ROAD SIGNS TO FINDING THE WILL OF GOD

1. The Bible

We can know the will of God through the Bible.

"Thy word is a lamp unto my feet, and a light unto my path" (Psalm 119:105, *KJV*).

The Bible is our authority when it comes to knowing God's will. As we read and study the Bible, we can know how God wants us to live in many situations. Look up the following verses and match them to the word or phrase found in the Bible that is God's will for our lives.

Love the Lord your God with all your heart, mind and soul.	James 1:26
Be thankful in all situations.	Matthew 6:33
Do not be conformed to this world.	Exodus 20:12
Seek first God's kingdom.	Exodus 20:14,15
Keep a tight rein on your tongue.	1 Corinthians 6:19,20
Do not commit adultery or steal.	1 Thessalonians 5:18
Honor your father and mother.	Romans 12:1,2
Honor God with your body.	Matthew 22:37

The list could go on and on. However, the Bible does not deal with every situation. For example, nowhere in Scripture will you find what college you should attend, or whether you should drive a VW or Chevrolet. When Scripture is silent on a subject, we look at other indicators to find out the will of God for our lives.

2. Counsel

Seek advice and counsel of others whom you respect. We all need to take the advice of the writer of Proverbs seriously. "Make plans by seeking advice" (Proverbs 20:18). "Where there is no guidance, the people fall; but in abundance of counselors there is victory" (Proverbs 11:14, *NASB*).

Whom can you go to for good, solid, sound advice?

....

....

You need people in your life, perhaps in your family or at your church, to whom you can go for advice and counsel. Weigh their thoughts heavily, but remember, you must ultimately make your own decisions.

3. Prayer

Prayer is another way of knowing the will of God. James tells us to ask God for wisdom, expecting Him to give it to us generously (see James 1:5-8).

Paul gave strong advice to his friends in the Philippian church when he wrote: "Don't worry about anything; instead, pray about everything; tell God your needs and don't forget to thank him for his answers" (Phil. 4:6, *TLB*).

IN THE WORD

a. What does Paul suggest you do instead of worrying about God's will?

....

....

....

b. Read Philippians 4:7. List the result of following Paul's instructions.

....

....

....

c. What are some specific areas in your life that you should be praying about?

....

....

4. Circumstances

At times, we can know the will of God through circumstances (see Proverbs 3:5,6; 16:9). Some people call it the open-door/closed-door policy of knowing circumstances. Be careful to look at events and situations over which you have no control as possible actions from God. Watch them carefully and slowly. Don't act impulsively on circumstances. Use the other methods of prayer, Bible reading and the wise counsel of others to help you see if the circumstances are from God.

a. What are a couple of circumstances over which you had no control that you believe God used to lead you to do His will?

....

....

....

b. Now, as a group, ask for volunteers to provide a problem or issue and ask the group to look at each problem or issue according to this road map. (For example: Dating a non-Christian or what church I should attend.)

....

....

....

 O WHAT?

1. Are there any issues in your life you need/want to give over to the will of God? List them.

....

....

....

2. Read Romans 12:1,2. How does it relate to your life and the will of God?

....

....

....

*T*HINGS TO THINK ABOUT

1. What does "Delight yourself in the Lord and he will give you the desires of your heart" (Psalm 37:4) mean?

....

....

2. Does God have the perfect job, person to marry, etc., picked out for you?

....

....

3. Sometimes you make a wrong decision. How does that fit into God's will?

....

....

4. Why is it so important to seek the advice of someone you respect?

....

....

5. Do you think there is ever more than one option that would fit into God's will?

....

....

....

PARENT PAGE

GOD'S WILL FOR MY LIFE
Matthew 6:25-34: Trust or Anxiety

1. Complete this sentence: When I hear the phrase, "Therefore I tell you, do not worry about your life," I feel:

☐ Confused

☐ Challenged

☐ Like a failure

☐ Confident of God's care for me

☐ Other ....

2. What is the most reassuring thought for you in this section of Scripture?

....

....

3. Complete this statement: The hardest thing for me in seeking God's kingdom and will first is:

....

....

4. What makes verse 34 one of the greatest pieces of advice Jesus ever gave to anyone?

....

....

5. Romans 12:1,2 and Colossians 3:1-4 have some important points in dealing with the aspect of living out God's will. What are those points?

....

....

Parent: Give at least two experiences in your life where you sensed God's will and intervention in your life.

....

....

....

Student: What are specific areas in your life which you hope God's will is a part of?

....

....

....

Session 9 "The Will of God" Date ....

187 © 1994 by Gospel Light. Permission to photocopy granted.

JESUS

KEY VERSES

"Jesus answered, 'I am the way and the truth and the life. No one comes to the Father except through me. If you really knew me, you would know my Father as well. From now on, you do know him and have seen him.'" John 14:6,7

BIBLICAL BASIS

Isaiah 42:1-9; 53:1-3;
Matthew 9:6; 16:13-16;
 25:34-40; 27:27-32;
Luke 2:52; 4:38-44;
John 1:1,14; 3:17; 4:25,26; 5:22,23;
 6:44-51; 8:58; 10:11-16,30; 14:6;
Philippians 2:5-11;
Hebrews 2:17,18; 4:15;
Revelation 1:8

THE BIG IDEA

The life and ministry of Jesus Christ is the most powerful and influential element of our Christian lives.

AIMS OF THIS SESSION

During this session you will guide students to:
• Examine the influence, claims and life of Jesus;
• Discover how His life and ministry relates to their lives;
• Implement a prayer asking Jesus to be real in their lives.

WARM UP

The Influence of Jesus Christ—
A story explaining how great Jesus' influence is.

TEAM EFFORT— JUNIOR HIGH/ MIDDLE SCHOOL

Show Me Jesus—
A look at artistic and scriptural descriptions of Jesus.

TEAM EFFORT— HIGH SCHOOL

Jesus: Name Above All Names—
Students discover many images of Christ.

IN THE WORD

Who Is This Man?—
A Bible study on who Jesus is.

THINGS TO THINK ABOUT (OPTIONAL)

Questions to get students thinking and talking about Jesus' identity.

PARENT PAGE

A tool to get the session into the home and allow parents and young people to discuss Jesus' place in their lives.

LEADER'S DEVOTIONAL

"[Jesus] would either be a lunatic—on level with the man who says he is a poached egg—or else he would be the Devil or Hell. You must make your choice. Either this man was, and is, the Son of God, or else a madman or something worse."—C. S. Lewis

"Who do you say that I am?" It is Jesus' question to Peter that still haunts believers and nonbelievers alike. Though certain New Testament scholars have given themselves the task of trying to deconstruct the life of Christ, Peter's response to Jesus offers everyone the hope of a transforming relationship with God. Jesus is the Messiah sent to save the world.

Helping young people develop a deeper walk with Jesus Christ affirms God's work in your life. By serving teenagers for the Kingdom, you are declaring to Jesus, "You are the Christ, the Son of the living God."

Helping someone to discover a personal friendship with Jesus is the best gift you could ever give someone. It's also a gift that you never want to ignore or neglect.

Before you rush out to prepare this lesson, spend some time with Jesus. Think about His presence in your life. How would you describe your relationship with Him right now? What struggles or frustrations do you need to give Him today?

Jesus Christ, the Son of the living God, wants you to know Him more and more. Everyday is a new chance to be freed of yesterday's regrets. Everyday is an opportunity to rest in His unconditional love for you. Though some people want to strip Jesus down to nothing, He wants to build into you how very essential He is to your life. (Written by Joey O'Connor.)

BIBLE *TUCK-IN* ™

Jesus

KEY VERSES

"Jesus answered, 'I am the way and the truth and the life. No one comes to the Father except through me. If you really knew me, you would know my Father as well. From now on, you do know him and have seen him.'" John 14:6,7

BIBLICAL BASIS

Isaiah 42:1-9; 53:1-3; Matthew 9:6; 16:13-16; 25:34-40; 27:27-32; Luke 2:52; 4:38-44; John 1:1,14; 3:17; 4:25,26; 5:22,23; 6:44-51; 8:58; 10:11-16,30; 14:6; Philippians 2:5-11; Hebrews 2:17,18; 4:15; Revelation 1:8

THE BIG IDEA

The life and ministry of Jesus Christ is the most powerful and influential element of our Christian lives.

WARM UP (5-10 MINUTES)

• Give each student a copy of "The Influence of Jesus Christ" on page 193 and a pen or pencil.
• Read aloud the story.
• As a whole group, discuss the students' responses.

Here is a man who was born in an obscure village, the child of a peasant woman. He grew up in another village. He worked in a carpenter shop until He was 30, and then for three years He traveled the country preaching. He never wrote a book. He never held an office. He never owned a home. He never had a family of His own. He never went to college. He never traveled more than two hundred miles from the place where He was born. He never did one of the things that usually accompany greatness. He had no credentials but Himself.

While still a young man, the tide of popular opinion turned against Him. His friends ran away. One of them denied Him. He was turned over to His enemies. He went through the mockery of a trial. He was nailed upon a cross between two thieves. His executioners gambled for the only piece of property He had on earth while He was dying. When he was dead He was taken down and laid in a borrowed grave through the pity of a friend.

Nineteen centuries have come and gone, and today He is the centerpiece of the human race and the leader of the column of progress.

I am far within the mark when I say that all the armies that ever marched, and all the navies that were ever built, and all the parliaments that ever sat, and all the kings that ever reigned, put together have not affected the life of man upon this earth as has that one solitary life.

How do you feel when you read about the effect of Jesus' life on our world? Mark the appropriate box and tell why.

☐ Overwhelmed
☐ Glad to be on His side
☐ Excited
☐ Not sure
☐ Other _____

--- Fold ---

4. Jesus as Savior. Read Matthew 9:6 and John 3:17.
   (He can forgive sins and was sent to save the world.)

5. Jesus as judge of the world. Read John 5:22,23.
   (The Father has entrusted all judgment to Him.)

6. Jesus as the Messiah. Read John 4:25,26.
   (He is the Messiah.)

7. Jesus is the God in the flesh. Read John 1:1,14.
   (He is God and lived as a man in this world.)

SO WHAT?

Jesus was fully God and fully man. Jesus knows what you are going through because He lived on this earth and completely identified with humankind. Jesus has the power to meet your needs because He is God. What important message is found in Hebrews 2:17,18 and Hebrews 4:15?

....

Write down three specific needs you have which Jesus can understand and with which He can help you.

1. ....

2. ....

3. ....

Which of Jesus' claims about Himself relates to your needs?

....

Offer a prayer of petition asking Jesus to be who He is in these areas of need.

THINGS TO THINK ABOUT (OPTIONAL)

• Use the questions on page 201 after or as a part of "In the Word."

1. What does "Jesus is fully God and fully human" mean to you?

....

2. What would the world say was the way, the truth and the life?

....

3. If you had one question about the claims of Jesus, what would it be?

....

PARENT PAGE

• Distribute page to parents.

TEAM EFFORT—JUNIOR HIGH/MIDDLE SCHOOL (15-20 MINUTES)

SHOW ME JESUS

- Have students describe what they believe Jesus looked like and why. Write their answers on a chalkboard, overhead transparency or paper.
- Display several different artists' renderings of Jesus. Discuss each picture and what you find out about Jesus from each picture.
- Read the following passages and determine what they tell you about Jesus: Isaiah 53:1-3; Matthew 27:27-32; Luke 2:52.

TEAM EFFORT—HIGH SCHOOL (15-20 MINUTES)

JESUS: NAME ABOVE ALL NAMES

- Divide students into groups of three or four.
- Give each student a copy of "Jesus: Name Above All Names" on page 195 and a pen or pencil.
- Students complete page.
- As a whole group, discuss students' answers.

What image of Christ do you find in each Scripture?

1. Philippians 2:5-11
   (Lord and Servant)
2. Matthew 25:34-40
   (King and Friend)
3. Isaiah 42:1-9
   (Suffering Servant)
4. John 10:11-16
   (Shepherd)
5. John 6:44-51
   (Teacher and Giver of eternal life)
6. Luke 4:38-44
   (Compassionate)
7. Matthew 16:13-16
   (Peter's confession)

IN THE WORD (25-30 MINUTES)

WHO IS THIS MAN?

- Assign the interview roles.
- Students conduct interview using the following questions. If possible, do this before the session so performers have an opportunity to rehearse.

1. What kind of clothes do you wear? Do you identify with a particular class of people (lower, middle or upper class, minority groups, etc.)?

2. Describe your family relationships.

3. What kind of people do you hang around with, and what do you talk about with them?

4. Where do you spend most of your time? What is your favorite hangout?

5. Are you a controversial figure? Why or why not?

6. How do you feel about the Church today? How do you get along with the religious leaders of our day?

7. What are your goals for the next 10 years?

8. How would you get your message out to as many people as possible?

9. What are you like politically?

10. If you had one wish for humankind what would it be?

- Have students state if they agree or disagree with the perception of Jesus in the interview and why.
- Give each student a copy of "Who Is This Man?" on page 197 and a pen or pencil, or display a copy using an overhead projector.

Let's take a look at the actual words Jesus used to describe Himself and see how we can better understand who He is by what He claimed about Himself. Determine what important truth Jesus says about Himself in each verse.

1. **Jesus is the way and the truth and the life. Read John 14:6.**
   (He is the one way to the Father.)
2. **Jesus is one with God. Read John 10:30.**
   (He is the same as the Father.)
3. **Jesus' preexistence. Read John 8:58 and Revelation 1:8.**
   (He always has been and always will be.)

Fold

WARM UP

THE INFLUENCE OF JESUS CHRIST

Here is a man who was born in an obscure village, the child of a peasant woman. He grew up in another village. He worked in a carpenter shop until He was 30, and then for three years He traveled the country preaching. He never wrote a book. He never held an office. He never owned a home. He never had a family of His own. He never went to college. He never traveled more than two hundred miles from the place where He was born. He never did one of the things that usually accompany greatness. He had no credentials but Himself.

While still a young man, the tide of popular opinion turned against Him. His friends ran away. One of them denied Him. He was turned over to His enemies. He went through the mockery of a trial. He was nailed upon a cross between two thieves. His executioners gambled for the only piece of property He had on earth while He was dying. When he was dead He was taken down and laid in a borrowed grave through the pity of a friend.

Nineteen centuries have come and gone, and today He is the centerpiece of the human race and the leader of the column of progress.

I am far within the mark when I say that all the armies that ever marched, and all the navies that were ever built, and all the parliaments that ever sat, and all the kings that ever reigned, put together have not affected the life of man upon this earth as has that one solitary life.[1]

How do you feel when you read about the effect of Jesus' life on our world? Mark the appropriate box and tell why.

☐ Overwhelmed
☐ Glad to be on His side
☐ Excited
☐ Not sure
☐ Other ....

Note

1. Public domain.

TEAM EFFORT

JESUS: NAME ABOVE ALL NAMES

What image of Christ do you find in each Scripture?

1. Philippians 2:5-11 ....

2. Matthew 25:34-40 ....

3. Isaiah 42:1-9 ....

4. John 10:11-16 ....

5. John 6:44-51 ....

6. Luke 4:38-44 ....

7. Matthew 16:13-16 ....

IN THE WORD

WHO IS THIS MAN?

Let's take a look at the actual words Jesus used to describe Himself and see how we can better understand who He is by what He claimed about Himself. Determine what important truth Jesus says about Himself in each verse.

1. Jesus is the way and the truth and the life. Read John 14:6.

....

....

2. Jesus is one with God. Read John 10:30.

....

....

3. Jesus' preexistence. Read John 8:58 and Revelation 1:8.

....

....

4. Jesus as Savior. Read Matthew 9:6 and John 3:17.

....

....

5. Jesus as judge of the world. Read John 5:22,23.

....

....

6. Jesus as the Messiah. Read John 4:25,26.

....

....

7. Jesus is the God in the flesh. Read John 1:1,14.

....

....

 **S**o WHAT?

Jesus was fully God and fully man. Jesus knows what you are going through because He lived on this earth and completely identified with humankind. Jesus has the power to meet your needs because He is God. What important message is found in Hebrews 2:17,18 and Hebrews 4:15?

....

....

Write down three specific needs you have which Jesus can understand and with which He can help you.

1. ....

2. ....

3. ....

Which of Jesus' claims about Himself relates to your needs?

....

....

....

Offer a prayer of petition asking Jesus to be who He is in these areas of need.

THINGS TO THINK ABOUT

1. What does "Jesus is fully God and fully human" mean to you?

....

....

....

2. What would the world say was the way, the truth and the life?

....

....

....

3. If you had one question about the claims of Jesus, what would it be?

....

....

....

PARENT PAGE

Here are two short but powerful illustrations about Jesus.

ANT STORY[1]

Once upon a time there was a colony of ants who were busy doing whatever ants do with their lives. God wanted to tell the ants of His love for them and His eternal home prepared for them. What was the very best way for God to communicate to those ants? The only possible way to speak to the ants was to become an ant and speak their language. So He did, and they believed.

1. How does this story relate to what Jesus did for us? Why is that significant?

....

....

2. What is your response to God's love for you?

....

....

LIAR, LUNATIC OR LORD?[2]

"I am trying here to prevent anyone saying the really foolish thing that people often say about Him: 'I'm ready to accept Jesus as a great moral teacher, but I don't accept His claim to be God.' That is the one thing we must not say. A man who was merely a man and said the sort of things Jesus said, would not be a great moral teacher. He would either be a lunatic—on a level with the man who says he is a poached egg—or else he would be the Devil or Hell. You must make your choice. Either this man was, and is, the Son of God, or else a madman or something worse."

Then Lewis adds, "You can shut Him up for a fool, you can spit at Him and kill Him as a demon; or you can fall at His feet and call Him Lord and God. But let us not come up with any patronizing nonsense about His being a great human teacher. He has not left that open to us. He did not intend to."

1. What are your personal thoughts about this statement made by C. S. Lewis?

....

....

2. What can your family do to make Jesus the Lord of your family?

....

....

....

Notes

1. Jim Burns, *Getting in Touch with God* (Eugene, OR: Harvest House Publishers, 1986), pp. 37-38. Used by permission.
2. C. S. Lewis, *Mere Christianity* (New York, NY: Macmillan, 1960), p. 56. Used by permission.

Session 10 "Jesus" Date ....

THE HOLY SPIRIT

KEY VERSE

"**B**ut I tell you the truth: It is for your good that I am going away. Unless I go away, the Counselor will not come to you; but if I go, I will send him to you." John 16:7

BIBLICAL BASIS

Matthew 5:6; 28:19;
John 14:16-18; 16:5-16;
Acts 1:8;
Romans 8:16; 12:1,2;
1 Corinthians 3:16; 6:18-20;
Galatians 5:16-26;
Ephesians 1:13; 5:18;
2 Timothy 2:19;
1 John 1:9

THE BIG IDEA

God sent the Holy Spirit to empower believers for guidance, revelation and conviction.

AIMS OF THIS SESSION

During this session you will guide students to:
• Examine what the Bible has to say about the Holy Spirit;
• Discover how the Holy Spirit can empower the believer;
• Implement a commitment to allow the Holy Spirit to empower their lives.

WARM UP

Find Someone—
Students find out about each other.

TEAM EFFORT— JUNIOR HIGH/ MIDDLE SCHOOL

A Rich Reservoir—
A story of God's power in Christians' lives.

TEAM EFFORT— HIGH SCHOOL

Fruit of the Spirit—
An inventory of the Spirit's evidence in students' lives.

IN THE WORD

The Holy Spirit—
A Bible study on who the Holy Spirit is and how He works.

THINGS TO THINK ABOUT (OPTIONAL)

Questions to get students thinking and talking about the Holy Spirit's work in their lives.

PARENT PAGE

A tool to get the session into the home and allow parents and young people to discuss the Holy Spirit.

Leader's Devotional

"In Michelangelo's famous painting on the ceiling of the Sistine Chapel, God is reaching out to Adam. Their hands never quite touch. The Holy Spirit is the missing touch of God."—James Bryan Smith

When the rock musician, Sting, sang, "We are spirits in the material world," he probably wasn't trying to make any bold theological statement about our true nature. However, he was right. The core of our being is spirit, and this material world we live in is only a temporary dwelling. As individuals designed by God, we were created to fellowship with Him for all of eternity.

God sent His Son, Jesus Christ, to bring us from being separated from God by sin back into fellowship with Him. Through the blood of Jesus, our spirit can be reunited in fellowship with God. It's the living presence of Jesus, God's Holy Spirit, that helps us to obey and understand God. Being empowered by God through His Spirit, we can do all things through Christ. Without His Spirit in our lives, we can do nothing. His Spirit is the empowering divine nature that frees us from the bondage of sin and death. It is on God's Spirit that we rely for help, guidance, protection, peace and security in this insecure world.

At times, we forget that God's Holy Spirit is as much a member of the Trinity as are the Father and the Son. The Father and the Son get a lot of attention, but the Holy Spirit tends to get left out of the picture. Don't we realize that it is the Holy Spirit who empowers us to walk in the steps of Jesus?

Let this study develop in you a greater love for the Holy Spirit. Ask yourself how you can yield your heart, mind and spirit to the Holy Spirit's work leading, guiding and protecting your every move. God deeply desires for you to walk in His Spirit. He wants the fruit of the Holy Spirit to nourish the young people He's placed in your care. Through the Holy Spirit, you have a reservoir of power in your life like nothing else in this material world. (Written by Joey O'Connor.)

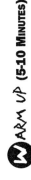

THE HOLY SPIRIT

KEY VERSE

"But I tell you the truth: It is for your good that I am going away. Unless I go away, the Counselor will not come to you; but if I go, I will send him to you." John 16:7

BIBLICAL BASIS

Matthew 5:6; 28:19; John 14:16-18; 16:5-16; Acts 1:8; Romans 8:16; 12:1,2; 1 Corinthians 3:16; 6:18-20; Galatians 5:16-26; Ephesians 1:13; 5:18; 2 Timothy 2:19; 1 John 1:9

THE BIG IDEA

God sent the Holy Spirit to empower believers for guidance, revelation and conviction.

WARM UP (5-10 MINUTES)

FIND SOMEONE

- Give each student a copy of "Find Someone" on page 209 and a pen or pencil.
- Students complete page.

Have someone initial each statement.

1. Find someone who uses Crest toothpaste. ....

2. Find someone who has three bathrooms in his or her house. ....

3. Find someone who has red hair. ....

4. Find someone who gets yelled at for spending too much time in the bathroom. ....

5. Find someone who has been inside the cockpit of an airplane. ....

6. Find someone who plays a guitar. ....

7. Find someone who likes frog legs. ....

8. Find someone who has used an outhouse. ....

9. Find a girl with false eyelashes on. ....

10. Find a guy who has gone water skiing and got up the first time. ....

11. Find someone who knows what "charisma" means. ....

12. Find someone who has been on a diet. ....

---

3. How does 1 Corinthians 6:18-20 help you understand in greater detail the indwelling of the Holy Spirit?

(Because the Holy Spirit lives within you, you are different. Your body is not your own.)

Take a moment to read this prayer. Then take a moment to make this prayer your own.

Spirit of the living God,
Take control of me;
Spirit of the living God,
Take control of me;
Spirit of the living God,
Take control of me;
Melt me! Mold me! Fill me! Use me!

C. The Holy Spirit gives you power to witness.

1. One of the last known sentences out of the mouth of Jesus is found in Acts 1:8.

What is the promise for you in this verse?

(You will receive power from the Holy Spirit.)

2. List three names of people with whom you would like to share God's love in the next month.

a. ....

b. ....

c. ....

D. The Holy Spirit gives you the assurance of your salvation.

1. What make Ephesians 1:13 a very important verse for your spiritual life?

(Your salvation was sealed by the Holy Spirit.)

2. What assurance is found in Romans 8:16?

(You are God's child.)

3. What challenge is found in 2 Timothy 2:19?

(Turn from wickedness.)

SO WHAT?

To conclude, read this last section and pray through each part of the heart preparation below and then pray to receive all the Holy Spirit has to offer your life.

In order to prepare your heart for the guiding and empowering of the Holy Spirit you must:

1. Desire to live for God (see Matthew 5:6).
2. Be willing to surrender and submit your will (life) to God (see Romans 12:1,2).
3. Confess your sins (see 1 John 1:9).
4. Be filled with the Spirit (see Ephesians 5:18).
5. Live by the Spirit (see Galatians 5:16).

THINGS TO THINK ABOUT (OPTIONAL)

- Use the questions on page 221 after or as a part of "In the Word."

1. How does it feel to know God dwells within you?

....

2. What does it mean to "walk in the Spirit"?

....

3. What keeps believers from submitting to God's Spirit?

....

4. What is the Holy Spirit doing in your life?

....

PARENT PAGE

- Distribute page to parents.

TEAM EFFORT—JUNIOR HIGH/MIDDLE SCHOOL (15-20 MINUTES)

A RICH RESERVOIR

- Give each student a copy of "A Rich Reservoir" on page 211 and a pen or pencil.
- Read aloud the story.
- As a whole group, discuss the students' responses.

1. How does the Holy Spirit of God empower believers to live the Christian life?

....

2. How does this story relate to your own need to tap into God's power?

....

TEAM EFFORT—HIGH SCHOOL (15-20 MINUTES)

FRUIT OF THE SPIRIT

- Give each student a copy of "Fruit of the Spirit" on page 213 and a pen or pencil.
- As a whole group, read the Scripture and answer the questions.
- Divide students into groups of three or four and have them complete the inventory.

Read Galatians 5:16-26 together in the group. Answer these questions and then break into groups to complete the inventory.

1. What are the results of walking in the Spirit, according to Galatians 5:23,24?

....

2. What are the works of the flesh found in Galatians 5:19-21?

....

Fruit of the Spirit Inventory

Below is a list of the fruit of the Spirit. Mark in the appropriate box how you feel you are doing in each area.

	Good	Average	Poor
Love	☐	☐	☐
Joy	☐	☐	☐
Peace	☐	☐	☐
Patience	☐	☐	☐
Kindness	☐	☐	☐
Goodness	☐	☐	☐
Faithfulness	☐	☐	☐
Gentleness	☐	☐	☐
Self-control	☐	☐	☐

Share in your group which areas you are doing well in and which areas could use work. This week ask God to help you in the areas in which you need work.

- Fold -

IN THE WORD (25-30 MINUTES)

THE HOLY SPIRIT

- Divide students into groups of three or four.
- Give each student a copy of "The Holy Spirit" on pages 215 to 219 and a pen or pencil.
- Students complete the page.

I. Who Is He and Why Did He Come?

Read John 16:5-16.

A. Who is the Holy Spirit?
1. Who does Jesus call the Holy Spirit in John 16:7?
(Counselor, Comforter or Helper.)
2. What is significant to you about the name Jesus gives the Holy Spirit in this verse?

B. Why did the Holy Spirit come?
List reasons for the Holy Spirit's coming from this teaching of Jesus.
1. Verse 7:
(For our good.)
2. Verse 8:
(Convicting the world of guilt.)
3. Verse 13:
(Speaking truth, God's Word and what is to come.)
4. Verse 14:
(Making God's plan known.)

II. The Work of the Holy Spirit

A. The Holy Spirit empowers and guides you to live the Christian life. In order to have the power of God working in our lives, we must surrender and submit ourselves to the control of the Holy Spirit of God.
1. In John 14:16,17, what does Jesus say He will ask the Father to give to those who love and obey Him?
(The Holy Spirit.)
2. What is His promise in John 14:18?
(He will not leave us.)
3. According to Ephesians 5:18, what command is given to believers?
(Be filled with the Spirit.)
4. How can you best surrender and submit yourself to God?

B. The Holy Spirit dwells inside believers.
1. Summarize 1 Corinthians 3:16.
(God lives in you.)
2. How can this verse give you great encouragement?

WARM UP

FIND SOMEONE

Have someone initial each statement.

1. Find someone who uses Crest toothpaste.
2. Find someone who has three bathrooms in his or her house.
3. Find someone who has red hair.
4. Find someone who gets yelled at for spending too much time in the bathroom.
5. Find someone who has been inside the cockpit of an airplane.
6. Find someone who plays a guitar.
7. Find someone who likes frog legs.
8. Find someone who has used an outhouse.
9. Find a girl with false eyelashes on.
10. Find a guy who has gone water skiing and got up the first time.
11. Find someone who knows what "charisma" means.
12. Find someone who has been on a diet.

TEAM EFFORT

A RICH RESERVOIR

A farmer and his wife, in the panhandle of Texas, had eked out a meager living in the dusty panhandle for 30 years when an impeccably dressed man, in a three-piece suit, driving a fancy car, came to their door. He told the farmer that he had good reason to believe there was a reservoir of oil underneath his property. If the farmer would allow the gentleman the right to drill, perhaps the farmer would become a wealthy man. The farmer stated emphatically that he didn't want anyone messing up his property and asked the gentleman to leave.

The next year, about the same time, the gentleman returned again with his nice clothes and another fancy car. The oilman pleaded with the farmer, and again the farmer said no. This same experience went on for the next eight years. During those eight years the farmer and his wife really struggled to make ends meet. Nine years after the first visit of the oilman, the farmer came down with a disease that put him in the hospital. When the gentleman arrived to plead his case for oil he spoke to the farmer's wife. Reluctantly she gave permission to drill.

Within a week huge oil rigs were beginning the process of drilling for oil. The first day nothing happened. The second day was filled with only disappointment and dust. But on the third day, right about noon, black bubbly liquid began to squirt up in the air. The oilman had found black gold, and the farmer and his wife were instantly millionaires.

You have a reservoir of power in your life. If you are a Christian, the Holy Spirit works in your life. You can tap into His power and live your life with resurrection power. The Holy Spirit will empower you to live life on a greater level, but you've got to tap into His power source just like the farmer needed to drill for oil.

1. How does the Holy Spirit of God empower believers to live the Christian life?

....

....

....

2. How does this story relate to your own need to tap into God's power?

....

....

....

....

TEAM EFFORT

FRUIT OF THE SPIRIT

Read Galatians 5:16-26 together in the group. Answer these questions and then break into groups to complete the inventory.

1. What are the results of walking in the Spirit, according to Galatians 5:23,24?

....

....

....

2. What are the works of the flesh found in Galatians 5:19-21?

....

....

....

Fruit of the Spirit Inventory

Below is a list of the fruit of the Spirit. Mark in the appropriate box how you feel you are doing in each area.

	Good	Average	Poor
Love	☐	☐	☐
Joy	☐	☐	☐
Peace	☐	☐	☐
Patience	☐	☐	☐
Kindness	☐	☐	☐
Goodness	☐	☐	☐
Faithfulness	☐	☐	☐
Gentleness	☐	☐	☐
Self-control	☐	☐	☐

Share in your group which areas you are doing well in and which areas could use work. This week ask God to help you in the areas in which you need work.

THE HOLY SPIRIT

I. Who Is He and Why Did He Come?

Read John 16:5-16.

A. Who is the Holy Spirit?

1. Who does Jesus call the Holy Spirit in John 16:7?

....

....

2. What is significant to you about the name Jesus gives the Holy Spirit in this verse?

....

....

B. Why did the Holy Spirit come?

List reasons for the Holy Spirit's coming from this teaching of Jesus.

1. Verse 7:..

....

2. Verse 8:..

....

3. Verse 13:..

....

4. Verse 14:..

....

II. The Work of the Holy Spirit

A. The Holy Spirit empowers and guides you to live the Christian life. In order to have the power of God working in our lives, we must surrender and submit ourselves to the control of the Holy Spirit of God.

1. In John 14:16,17, what does Jesus say He will ask the Father to give to those who love and obey Him?

....

....

2. What is His promise in John 14:18?

....

....

....

IN THE WORD

3. According to Ephesians 5:18, what command is given to believers?

....

....

....

4. How can you best surrender and submit yourself to God?

....

....

B. The Holy Spirit dwells inside believers.
   1. Summarize 1 Corinthians 3:16.

....

....

....

   2. How can this verse give you great encouragement?

....

....

   3. How does 1 Corinthians 6:18-20 help you understand in greater detail the indwelling of the Holy
      Spirit?

Take a moment to read this prayer. Then take a moment to make this prayer your own.

> Spirit of the living God,
> Take control of me;
> Spirit of the living God,
> Take control of me;
> Spirit of the living God.
> Take control of me;
> Melt me! Mold me! Fill me! Use me!

C. The Holy Spirit gives you power to witness.
   1. One of the last known sentences out of the mouth of Jesus is found in Acts 1:8. What is the promise
      for you in this verse?

....

....

   2. List three names of people with whom you would like to share God's love in the next month.
      a. ....
      b. ....
      c. ....

D. The Holy Spirit gives you the assurance of your salvation.

1. What make Ephesians 1:13 a very important verse for your spiritual life?

....

....

2. What is the assurance found in Romans 8:16?

....

....

3. What is the challenge found in 2 Timothy 2:19?

....

....

 **$o WHAT?**

To conclude, read this last section and pray through each part of the heart preparation below and then pray to receive all the Holy Spirit has to offer your life.

In order to prepare your heart for the guiding and empowering of the Holy Spirit you must:

1. Desire to live for God.

   "Blessed are those who hunger and thirst for righteousness, for they will be filled" (Matthew 5:6).

2. Be willing to surrender and submit your will (life) to God.

   "Therefore, I urge you, brothers, in view of God's mercy, to offer your bodies as living sacrifices, holy and pleasing to God—this is your spiritual act of worship. Do not conform any longer to the pattern of this world, but be transformed by the renewing of your mind. Then you will be able to test and approve what God's will is—his good, pleasing and perfect will" (Romans 12:1,2).

3. Confess your sins.

   "If we confess our sins, he is faithful and just and will forgive us our sins and purify us from all unrighteousness" (1 John 1:9).

4. Be filled with the Spirit.

   "Do not get drunk on wine, which leads to debauchery. Instead, be filled with the Spirit" (Ephesians 5:18).

5. Live by the Spirit.

   "So I say, live by the Spirit, and you will not gratify the desires of the sinful nature" (Galatians 5:16).

T HINGS TO THINK ABOUT

1. How does it feel to know God dwells within you?

....

....

....

2. What does it mean to "walk in the Spirit"?

....

....

....

3. What keeps believers from submitting to God's Spirit?

... .

....

....

4. What is the Holy Spirit doing in your life?

....

....

....

....

PARENT PAGE

THE HOLY SPIRIT

Look up each Scripture and match it with the phrase below.

The Holy Spirit is a part of the Triune God.	John 16:13
The Holy Spirit gives us the power to witness.	John 14:16,17
The Holy Spirit will guide believers in all things.	Acts 1:8
The Holy Spirit glorifies Jesus Christ.	Matthew 28:19
The Holy Spirit is our Counselor (Comforter, Helper).	John 16:14

The Trinity

Try an experiment in the kitchen with the various properties of water. Demonstrate the three-in-one effect of showing water as a liquid, frozen solid and a steam vapor.

Then discuss how this illustration relates to the relationship of God-Jesus-Holy Spirit. (You can also use the three parts of a light. A switch, the wiring and the bulb.)

Now have each person name a way the Holy Spirit of God has affected his or her life.

....

....

....

....

....

THE CHURCH

KEY VERSE

"The body is a unit, though it is made up of many parts; and though all its parts are many, they form one body. So it is with Christ."
1 Corinthians 12:12

BIBLICAL BASIS

Psalm 95:6-7; 118:24; 133:1;
Proverbs 18:24; 29:18;
Matthew 10:7,8,34;
1 John 5:39;
Romans 12:10;
1 Corinthians 12:12-31; 13:3;
1 John 4:7

THE BIG IDEA

The Church is the Body of Christ made up of all believers with a variety of gifts.

AIMS OF THIS SESSION

During this session you will guide students to:
• Examine the description of the Church in 1 Corinthians 12;
• Discover their place in their church;
• Get more involved in their church using their God-given talents and gifts.

WARM UP

Me and the Church—
Students share their thoughts on church.

TEAM EFFORT— JUNIOR HIGH/ MIDDLE SCHOOL

The Life-Saving Station—
A story explaining the purpose of the Church.

TEAM EFFORT— HIGH SCHOOL

Is It or Isn't It?—
Teens determine what the Church is.

IN THE WORD

The Church: The Body of Christ—
A Bible study on the roles people have in the Church.

THINGS TO THINK ABOUT (OPTIONAL)

Questions to get students thinking and talking about the Church.

PARENT PAGE

A tool to get the session into the home and allow parents and young people to discuss involvement in their church.

LEADER'S DEVOTIONAL

"Teenagers are another story. For them, charming or appealingly angst-ridden smokers can serve as missionaries for tobacco. Three million of the nation's 46 million smokers are teenagers, consuming nearly a billion packs of cigarettes a year; each day an estimated 3,000 teens take their first puff."—"Hollywood Goes Up in Smoke," *People*, September, 1994

Missionaries for tobacco? Instead of puffing their lives away and seeing their lives go up in smoke, you have the exciting chance to help teenagers understand their role in the Body of Christ. When young people discover that they are ambassadors for God, their whole lives take on a new dimension.

For every student who confesses Jesus as Lord, each one has spiritual gifts just waiting to be used for God's glory. Many young people have a negative view of church. To them, church is dull, boring and irrelevant. Perhaps it's because they've always been on the outside looking in? Maybe nobody has ever taken the time to help them discover their spiritual gifts? Can you imagine what this world would be like if every student in your youth ministry understood their role in the Body of Christ?

You can help teenagers become missionaries for God by helping them see that God wants to use them to influence their families and friends for His Kingdom. This lesson will be a great primer to develop leadership in your youth ministry. The most powerful student ministries are the ones with strong student leadership. Students have the chance to discover that the Church isn't a thing or place, but it's Christ living out His presence in their lives. Though the smoking statistics for young people may be on the rise, God wants you to set your students on fire for Christ. (Written by Joey O'Connor.)

THE CHURCH

KEY VERSES

"The body is a unit, though it is made up of many parts; and though all its parts are many, they form one body. So it is with Christ." 1 Corinthians 12:12

BIBLICAL BASIS

Psalm 95:6-7; 118:24; 133:1; Proverbs 18:24; 29:18; Matthew 10:7,8,34; John 5:39; Romans 12:10; 1 Corinthians 12:12-31; 13:3; 1 John 4:7

THE BIG IDEA

The Church is the Body of Christ made up of all believers with a variety of gifts.

WARM UP (5-10 MINUTES)

ME AND THE CHURCH

- Divide students into pairs.
- Display a copy of "Me and the Church" on page 229 using an overhead projector.
- Students complete statements.

  My first memory of church is:

  When I think of church I usually feel:

  The best thing about church is:

  The worst thing about church is:

  If I were a pastor I would:

TEAM EFFORT—JUNIOR HIGH/MIDDLE SCHOOL (15-20 MINUTES)

THE LIFE-SAVING STATION

- Divide students into groups of three or four.
- Display a copy of "The Life-Saving Station" on pages 231 and 233 using an overhead projector.
- Students answer questions.

  1. When was the life-saving station most effective?

- Fold -

2. How are the roles related to each other?

SO WHAT?

According to 1 Corinthians 12:12-31, what are some roles you could have in your church?

What steps can you personally take to be more active in your church and youth group?

THINGS TO THINK ABOUT (OPTIONAL)

- Use the questions on page 243 after or as a part of "In the Word."
  1. Why do we call Jesus the head of the Church?

2. How would you describe the Church to a friend?

3. What are ways your youth group or you individually can improve the life and ministry of your church?

PARENT PAGE

- Distribute page to parents.

2. Where did the life-saving station go wrong?

3. How is the Church like a life-saving station? What is the purpose of the Church?

4. If you don't like the Church as it is now, what alternatives do you have?

5. How can the problems that the people of the life-saving station experienced be avoided in the Church? What should the members of the life-saving station have done?

6. Is being a part of the Church necessary to being a Christian?

7. Now for the big question! Since you are an important part of the Church (Body of Christ), what can you be doing to help make your Church or fellowship a better place?

TEAM EFFORT—HIGH SCHOOL (15-20 MINUTES)

IS IT OR ISN'T IT?

• Have a copy of "Is It or Isn't It?" on page 235 for each group. Cut apart phrases.
• On a chalkboard or newsprint, write "The Church Is..." on one side and "The Church Isn't..." on the other.
• Divide students into groups of three or four.
• Give each group a set of phrases and tape.
• Students place phrases under the proper headings.
• Have students add their own phrases to each heading.

- - - - - Fold - - - - -

The Church Is...

people who make a lot of mistakes while trying to serve God.

a place for hurting people to find comfort and help.

something set up by God to help His people through life.

a group of people sharing a common faith and hope in Jesus Christ.

a group of people gifted by God to serve Him together.

The Church Isn't...

a place for old people to gather and listen to a dull sermon.

a place for good people to meet together and be happy about their goodness.

an old building with stained-glass windows.

a bunch of cranky people who want to keep teenagers from having a good time.

the place where God lives.

IN THE WORD (25-30 MINUTES)

THE CHURCH: THE BODY OF CHRIST

• Assign skit roles.
• Give each character a copy of "The Church: The Body of Christ" on pages 237 and 239.
• Characters perform skit.
• Give each student a copy of "The Church: The Body of Christ" on pages 237 to 239 and a pen or pencil.
• As a whole group, complete page.

Read 1 Corinthians 12:12-31.

1. What different roles can people have in the Church?

WARM UP

ME AND THE CHURCH

My first memory of church is:

....

....

....

When I think of church I usually feel:

....

....

....

The best thing about church is:

....

....

....

The worst thing about church is:

....

....

....

If I were a pastor I would:

....

....

....

TEAM EFFORT

THE LIFE-SAVING STATION[1]

On a dangerous seacoast where shipwrecks often occur there was once a crude little life-saving station. The building was just a hut, and there was only one boat but the few devoted members kept a constant watch over the sea, and with no thought for themselves went out day and night tirelessly searching for the lost. Some of those who were saved, and various others in the surrounding area, wanted to become associated with the station and give of their time and money and effort for the support of its work. New boats were bought and new crews trained. The little life-saving station grew.

Some of the members of the life-saving station were unhappy that the building was so crude and poorly equipped. They felt that a more comfortable place should be provided as the first refuge of those saved from the sea. They replaced the emergency cots with beds and put better furniture in the enlarged building. Now the life-saving station became a popular gathering place for its members, and they decorated it as a sort of club. Fewer members were now interested in going to sea on life-saving missions, so they hired lifeboat crews to do this work. The life-saving motif still prevailed in this club's decoration, and there was a liturgical lifeboat in the room where the club initiations were held. About this time a large ship was wrecked off the coast, and the hired crews brought in boatloads of cold, wet and half-drowned people. They were dirty and sick and some of them had black skin and some had yellow skin. The beautiful new club was in chaos. So the property committee immediately had a shower house built outside the club where victims of shipwrecks could be cleaned up before coming inside.

At the next meeting, there was a split in the club membership. Most of the members wanted to stop the club's life-saving activities as being unpleasant and a hindrance to the normal social life of the club. Some members insisted upon life-saving as their primary purpose and pointed out that they were still called a life-saving station. But they were finally voted down and told that if they wanted to save lives of all the various kinds of people who were shipwrecked in those waters, they could begin their own life-saving station down the coast. They did.

As the years went by, the new station experienced the same changes that had occurred in the old. It evolved into a club, and yet, another life-saving station was founded. History continued to repeat itself, and if you visit that sea coast today, you will find a number of exclusive clubs along that shore. Shipwrecks are frequent in those waters, but most of the people drown.

1. When was the life-saving station most effective?

....

....

2. Where did the life-saving station go wrong?

....

....

3. How is the Church like a life-saving station? What is the purpose of the Church?

....

Team Effort

4. If you don't like the Church as it is now, what alternatives do you have?

....

....

5. How can the problems that the people of the life-saving station experienced be avoided in the Church? What should the members of the life-saving station have done?

....

....

....

6. Is being a part of the Church necessary to being a Christian?

....

....

7. Now for the big question! Since you are an important part of the Church (Body of Christ), what can you be doing to help make your Church or fellowship a better place?

....

....

....

Note

1. *Ideas 5-8* (El Cajon, CA: Youth Specialties, 1980), p. 78. Used by permission.

 *TEAM EFFORT*

IS IT OR ISN'T IT?[1]

The Church Is...

✂

people who make a lot of mistakes while trying to serve God.

✂

a place for hurting people to find comfort and help.

✂

something set up by God to help His people through life.

✂

a group of people sharing a common faith and hope in Jesus Christ.

✂

a group of people gifted by God to serve Him together.

✂

The Church Isn't...

✂

a place for old people to gather and listen to a dull sermon.

✂

a place for good people to meet together and be happy about their goodness.

✂

an old building with stained-glass windows.

✂

a bunch of cranky people who want to keep teenagers from having a good time.

✂

the place where God lives.

✂

Note

1. *What Is the Church?* (Loveland, CO: Group Publishing, Inc., 1992), pp.71-74. Used by permission.

THE CHURCH

IN THE WORD

THE CHURCH: THE BODY OF CHRIST

The Body Life Skit[1]

Each character should wear a sign or T-shirt that identifies the part they play. The reader should have a Bible.

Characters:

Reader

Nose (shy, sneezes a lot)

Foot (wearing big shoes)

Ear (wearing earphones)

Eye (wearing big glasses)

Head (acting conceited)

The skit begins with the body parts in a huddle.

Reader: I'll be reading selections from 1 Corinthians, chapter 12. "The body is a unit, though it is made up of many parts (the body parts spread apart and begin showing off their individual talents as the Reader continues), and though all its parts are many, they form one body. So it is with Christ. For we were all baptized by one Spirit into one body—whether Jews or Greeks, slave or free—and we were all given the one Spirit to drink. Now the body is not made up of one part but of many. If the foot should say..."

Foot: "Because I am not a hand, I do not belong to the body!"

Reader: "It would not for that reason cease to be part of the body."

Foot: Oh, yes, it would. I mean, I can go places, give the elderly rides to church, and drive Meals on Wheels. But I can't give a lot of money like a hand could, or cook the best dish at the covered dish supper like a hand could. Maybe I'm just not needed around here!

Reader: "And if the ear should say..."

Ear: "Because I am not an eye, I do not belong to the body."

Reader: "It would not for that reason cease to be part of the body."

Ear: Oh yeah? I mean, I can hear and understand a good sermon pretty well, but I can't seem to see places where anyone needs help like an eye could. What good is it to be able to hear and understand if you can't see to do anything? Maybe I'm just not needed around here!

Reader: "If the whole body were an eye, where would the sense of hearing be? If the whole body were an ear, where would the sense of smell be?...The eye cannot say to the hand..."

Eye: I don't need you, hand! I mean, I'm the most important part around here after all. That's pretty obvious. Anyone can see that without me, this body's just stumbling around in the dark. What good are you, hand?

Reader: "And the head cannot say to the feet..."

Head: Well, I don't need either of you. I can think and reason and make all the important decisions without any help at all from you guys. I'm the brains of this outfit.

Reader: (At this point, all the parts of the body begin arguing with each other so that the Reader must plead with them to stop. The nose moves off to the side and begins to cry.) "On the con-

IN THE WORD

trary, those parts of the body that seem to be weaker are indispensable, and the parts that we think are less honorable we treat with special honor....God has combined the members of the body...so that there should be no division in the body..." (The arguing gets progressively worse.) "...but that its parts should have equal concern for each other...." Oh, I give up! (Reader walks away exasperated.)

Ear: Hey wait a minute. Listen! I hear someone crying. (Everyone finally gets quiet.)

Eye: Look, it's _____ (use the name of the person playing the nose). Poor guy, I wonder what's wrong.

Head: I've got an idea! We could go over there and find out.

Ear: Hey, I like the sound of that idea!

Head: (Acting proud) Of course it's a good idea.

Eye: But how could we get there?

Foot: I could take you, I suppose....(General agreement. Everyone lines up behind the Foot, forms a train, and goes over to the Nose.)

Ear: (to nose) We heard you crying and we're kind of worried about you. Can we help somehow?

Nose: I don't know. I get so lonely sometimes. I wish I had some friends. But who wants to be friends with someone whose greatest talent is sniffing out trouble!

Eye: Well, I don't know about the rest of this crew, but it seems to me that we've got some trouble that needs sniffing out. (Everyone looks at the Head. Head looks sheepish).

Head: Well...maybe you're right....

Foot: You just come with us. We're not perfect yet, but when we all work together, we can do a lot of good after all. (Body parts form a line with arms around each others' shoulders.)

Reader: (stepping in front to read.) "If one part suffers, every part suffers with it; if one part is honored, every part rejoices with it. Now you are the body of Christ...."

Read 1 Corinthians 12:12-31.
1. What different roles can people have in the Church?

....

....

....

2. How are the roles related to each other?

....

....

....

....

So What?

1. According to 1 Corinthians 12:12-31, what are some roles you could have in your church?

....

....

....

2. What steps can you personally take to be more active in your church and youth group?

....

....

....

....

Note

1. Bill McNabb and Steven Mabry, *Teaching the Bible Creatively to Young People* (Grand Rapids, MI: Zondervan, 1990), pp.158-159. Used by permission.

THINGS TO THINK ABOUT

1. Why do we call Jesus the head of the Church?

....

....

2. How would you describe the Church to a friend?

....

....

3. What are ways your youth group or you individually can improve the life and ministry of your church?

....

....

....

PARENT PAGE

YOUR CHURCH'S JOB DESCRIPTION

In the space below, write a job description for your church. Rank its five major job responsibilities. Read these Bible passages to get you started: Psalm 95:6-7; 118:24; 133:1; Proverbs 18:24; 29:18; Matthew 10:7,8,34; John 5:39; Romans 12:10; 1 Corinthians 13:3; 1 John 4:7.

Your church's job responsibilities:

1. ....
2. ....
3. ....
4. ....
5. ....

Now imagine you're applying for a job at your church. Rank your five top talents or skills and write them below.

My five top talents or gifts:

1. ....
2. ....
3. ....
4. ....
5. ....

Now match your skills with the five most important job responsibilities of your church.

Do any match?

....

....

....

How can you as a family volunteer your service at your church?

....

....

....

You and your church may need each other more than you think.

Session 12 "The Church" Date ....